CW00422243

FRANNY & CONNOR WRITE A COOKBOOK

CREATED BY:

FRANCESCA CHILCOTE & CONNOR HOGAN

ALONG WITH THEIR AUDIENCE

CONCEPT BY: HANNAH CABBELL

DESIGN AND LAYOUT BY: DEBI BELT

First Edition August 2023

Design Concept by Hannah Cabbell

Book Design and Illustrations by Debi Belt

ISBN 9781088169094

Published by Ingram Spark

TABLE OF CONTENTS

INTRODUCTION

I have never cooked a frozen lasagna
What do you mean he only eats tuna casserole?
No no, baby, you're boiling the eggs all wrong!
And that's how you make a Domin-omelette.

Most of our stories start with food. In fact, we were the pioneers of eat-acting—or acting while eating. In the spring of 2009, Connor directed Francesca in a production of Anton Chekhov's "The Proposal". In the world of the play, Franny played Natalya, a foolish younger girl who is answering the marriage proposal of her neighbor, Lomov. While Fran's talent was there, Connor knew that there was something missing dramaturgically.

"You need something that makes you uglier," Connor said. "You're too pretty right now."

Fran furrowed her brow and adjusted her ponytail. "I could eat."

The next rehearsal, Connor had strategically hidden glazed Honey Buns around the rehearsal room. They were ninety-nine cents a piece and Connor had received a small props budget from their undergraduate theatre department. The Honey Buns were so instrumental in the creation process for "The Proposal" that Francesca gained fifteen pounds by the time it closed.

Ever since then, we've been collaborators both on stage and in the kitchen. Well, in the kitchen, sometimes we are rivals. Vying for control, as one pair of arms reaches over the other person who's actively trying to sauté something on the stove top. Questioning the other: "Oh is that how you do it?" Playing little pranks like moving the other's cutting board across the room. Or dropping a whole bottle of olive oil all over the floor and using a roommate's clean towel to sop up the whole greasy mess. In our time together, we've gone through a thousand messes, chopped thousands of cloves of garlic and made a thousand delicious dishes for our families and friends. In doing so, we learned that rivals can still be collaborators!

Because more often than not, we're looking for a hand to chop an onion or drain a pasta or stir a sauce. We love to cook for others and

have done so since Francesca first made our whole group of friends a chicken Parmesan dinner. Connor served as sous chef and the rest was history. Whenever you invited Franny or Connor over, you knew that we'd eventually get hungry, raid your pantry and cook everyone in the house a delicious meal. Because the one thing we love more than food is sharing that food with those we love.

Yet during the early days of the COVID-19 pandemic, we were not often able to partake in this most human activity of sharing a meal. Franny often says that there is an Italian saying *A me, chi sei? Non mai abbiamo mangiato insieme.* which, for the Connors of the world,

translates to "Who are you to me? We've never eaten together." For us, every human interaction happens better over a meal—whether it be brunch time bites or bigger dinner plates. While we were separated, we still craved each other's friendship and love in this particular way.

These two loves—of each other and of food—is what sparked the idea for *Dinner! Franny and Connor Write a Cookbook*. As most of our schemes start, it began as a joke: "What if we just video call someone, look through their pantry and yell frantic directions at them to cook a meal based only on the things they have in their house?" And well, dear reader, that's exactly what we did. With nothing but each other and a pro Zoom account, we dove head first into the world of digital pandemic theater.

We performed "Dinner!" thirty-six times for thirty-six different households across the country. From Philadelphia and D.C., we broadcast into the homes of folks experiencing isolation, loss, joy in solitude, new relationships, old bonds and a consistent hunger for human connection. In these interactions, we learned so much about how these folks relate to food and how it informs their own personal history. We cooked almost every kind of thing you can imagine—from Samuel and Ramon's Bodega Poke Bowls constructed solely from items purchased at a convenience store to Kari's Slamming Moon Yay, a cheeky brunch time Salmon Meuniere. Among the salts and spices of these folks' cabinets, we found stories that tickled more than just our taste buds. We've shared these stories along with these recipes here with you to remind you of the worlds that can be conjured with the right set of ingredients and the right company to share them with.

That is at the heart of what we do as amateur cooks: sharing something new with those we love. Everything we have learned about cooking springs from a place of admiration for ingredients, what they can become and the great meals you can share with friends. What you will find here are thirty-three recipes devised from the pantries of folks just like you. While the contents of your pantry might differ, your goal stays the same: to create something where there wasn't anything before.

As you try out some of these tasty creations, imagine these folks in their own kitchen roasting their own red pepper over an open flame. In that moment, you're bound together by the crackle of the fire and the release of the steam. We, Franny and Connor, share in that with you too. The ingredients listed here are just suggestions for you in your own culinary open canvas. While you chop and mince, consider: what flavors do you like? For example, Franny craves those acidy hits that tingle your pallet in a dish. While Connor is more earthy, he appreciates the silky smooth texture of a fatty and creamy dish. But how do you like it? And how can you take what we've learned here and make it a meal that can fully satiate you? Oh, and don't forget a friend because no one should ever eat alone.

BRUNCH!
BRUNCH!
BRUNCH!

Okay, so we know that the title of this book is called Dinner! but our favorite meal is truly brunch. I mean, when else is it socially acceptable to pound back three mimosas while scarfing down a delicious eggs Benedict? You see, we have a saying—"excess is our forte." And nowhere could we be more excessive than guiding our audiences in the creation of these brunch meals! In these recipes, you'll find stories of new beginnings, of old friends and not just one but two recipes for shakshuka. Brunch really can be as gussied up or as casual as you want, so go wild when you're recreating these.

Want a quick tip for making almost anything into brunch? Top any leftovers with an egg and you're good to go. Order takeout last night and you're trying to figure out what to do with a leftover curry? Put an egg on it and mop it all up with some toasted naan bread. Leftover spaghetti from a night of dinner with your in-laws? Throw a poached egg on top of there with some Parmesan and freshly cracked pepper and dive into a mountain of carby tomatoey egg goodness. Heck! Tear up some leftover pizza, mix it with a few eggs and make yourself the dreaded Dominomelette—a Domino's omelette.

This trick was first revealed to us in college by our perennially hungover friend Greg. While it all might have started as a way to fend off a nasty hangover, we now pass it along to you in hopes that you'll turn it into culinary greatness!

THE LAST GARDEN OMELETTE IN QUEENS

BY FRANNY & CONNOR & CARL & KATHY

As a boy, Carl looked forward to Saturday night sleepovers with his grandpa every week. You see, his Grandpa owned the last garden in Queens and it was magic. In the 1920s, Queens was mostly farmland. There were even pigs! After WWII, however, these fecund estates slowly started to disappear. His grandpa, Nathan, had the last farm left on 73rd Street in Jackson Heights.

The land was quite literally grandfathered in. On his farm, he grew all sorts of beautiful vegetables: asparagus, tomatoes, shallots, carrots, cabbage, garlic, and arugula. Every Saturday morning, Carl, his brother and his cousin would walk the 15 minutes to Grandpa's house, and help him work the land of the New York City borough. They planted seeds, weeded the lot, and picked the vegetables. Carl's favorite part was playing in the dirt. After their chores, they reaped the fruit of their labors, and were rewarded with beautiful fresh produce which Nathan would turn into a satisfying garden omelette. Nathan also owned a luncheonette by Giants stadium which made him an expert omelet flipper.

As an adult, it became harder for Carl to find the fresh in a Fresh Garden Omelette. Fortuitously, he met Kathy, who grew up in rural southwestern Pennsylvania. She knew how to cultivate the beautiful herbs and spices that added an extra lift to this dish. Rosemary, oregano, thyme, and basil, all grew to success in Kathy's garden. They've brought this perfect marriage of plump, fresh produce, and crisp, flavorful herbs in this omelette together for you to enjoy.

WHAT YOU'LL NEED:

2 to 4 asparagus stalks, chopped into ¼ inch pieces
1 shallot, diced
½ pint of cherry tomatoes
1 tbs olive oil
2 tbs butter
4-5 large eggs
½ cup mozzarella cheese, shredded
¼ tsp red pepper flakes
½ tsp garlic powder
½ tsp of oregano
salt and pepper

WHAT YOU'LL NEED TO DO:

1. Prep your veggies. Chop your asparagus into ½ to 1 inch pieces. Dice your shallot. Half your cherry tomatoes. Set aside.
2. In a large skillet, heat olive oil over medium. Lightly saute the asparagus with the shallot until it's bright green and fragrant. Remove from the pan and set aside.
3. Crack the eggs into a bowl and whisk together. Add salt, pepper, red pepper flakes, garlic powder and oregano. Whisk until mixture is a uniform color and consistency.
4. In the same skillet you cooked the asparagus in, heat two tablespoons of butter until the whole pan is full and foamy. Turn down the heat. Pour in half the egg mixture to coat the bottom of the pan. As the edges begin to cook up, pull them into the center with a rubber spatula and allow more of the liquid egg to seep into the edges.
5. Okay, I am going to be real with you here: omelettes are anxiety inducing. Do you know the phrase 'you've got to break a few eggs to make an omelette?' Well guess what? That phrase is true. You might go through dozens and dozens of eggs until you perfect your omelette technique. And that's okay. Cause if you mess up, you can just turn it into an equally tasty scramble. Be kind to yourself if your omelette turns to a scramble. You'll get it eventually.
6. Once it looks cooked, sprinkle the veggies and cheese on one half of the pan. Flip the other half over top, and cook for a few moments. Remove from heat.

This recipe makes two omelettes so, if you mess up the first one, you have more eggs to try again!

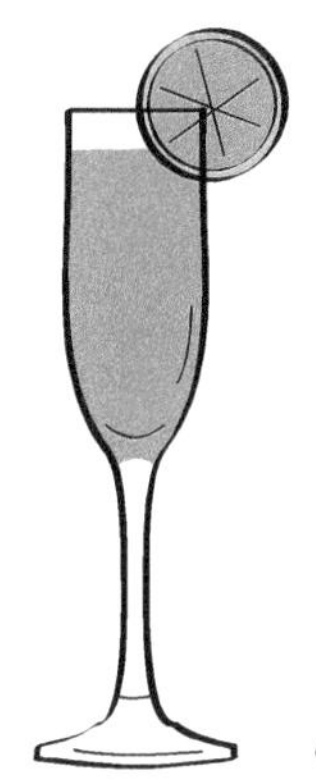

BY FRANNY & CONNOR & ANNA

Due to the pandemic, Anna and her husband Aaron had found themselves back in their home state of Kansas. You know, the one that looks like a zoom window with a hand blocking the corner? They'd been traveling back into the heart of the country in search of safe harbor from COVID 19. Little did they know that they'd find a familiar coastal friend, the leafy greens of kale, waiting for them right in their ancestral home. You see, kale was first introduced to the denizens of Kansas City through a popular national pizza chain because it was the ruffly leaves of kale that served as a garnish at Pizza Hut. Before long, however, Kansans couldn't get enough of the stuff, and it's now as popular in the middle of the country as it is in a chopped up bowl from a DC Sweetgreen. And it's this veggie that takes on a new life when prepared in Anna's delicious Shakshuka.

This veggie forward shakshuka will prepare you for a hearty day of brainy dissertation prep. Now, you might think that you need to escape your home to find success, but, just like a kale garnish at

Pizza Hut, self-actualization can happen where you least expect it. Colorful vegetables pop against the whites of eggs gathered from the Mennonite farmers down the road. A spicy bite leads to a savory one as you consider what your life has become since you left home. This dish brings a little bit of Cali to Kansas. Even your mom with a broken foot will love it! Especially if you serve it with crunchy crunchy bread. A pickled jalapeño tahini sauce is the perfect pairing for this dish, and will even mask the flavor of tomatoes from your nightshade hating husband. Re-find yourself with this squatshuka, no matter where you hail from in this complicated and complex country.

WHAT YOU'LL NEED:

FOR THE SHAKSHUKA

20 oz can of whole peeled tomatoes
2 carrots, peeled and diced
1 onion, yellow or white
1 bunch of kale
1 green pepper, diced
1 tsp golden milk spice
(or other spices such as cumin, chili, oregano, turmeric, etc)
1 tsp paprika
½ tsp cayenne
salt and pepper
4 large eggs

FOR THE TAHINI SAUCE

4 radishes, chopped
a few slices of pickled jalapenos
2 tbs of tahini
1 tbs olive oil
juice of one lemon
1 date, diced
½ bunch cilantro, chopped

crusty bread

jalapenos on the side

NOTES

WHAT YOU'LL NEED TO DO:

1. Preheat your oven to 375°.
2. Chop up your carrot, onion, and green pepper as chunky as you like. Separate the kale stalks from the leaves, and dice them up small.
3. Heat a big, oven safe pan on medium heat, throw in the onions and kale stalks and cook down, then continue to add in whatever vegetables you like, going from hardest (green peppers and carrots) to softest (garlic, shallots). Add salt and pepper.
4. Once all the vegetables are nice and soft, pour in the tomatoes and crush up using your spatula. Add in your spices here. Let the mixture simmer until it reduces and grows saucy.
5. With the back of a spoon, make divots in the tomato mixture for the eggs and break eggs into the holes. Put the pan into the oven.
6. Meanwhile, mix the tahini with the olive oil and juice of one lemon until well combined. Next, fold in the diced dates, jalapeños and cilantro. Set aside.
7. Check on the eggs. Remove them when the whites are set and the yolks are still runny. Top with tahini sauce, jalapeños, and serve with crusty bread.

*If you don't have an oven safe pan, you can move the shakshuka into a baking pan and put the eggs in there.

SHAKSHUKA 2. THE RE SEASONING

BY FRANNY & CONNOR & TONY

Shakshuka. Just say it out loud—shakshuka. When I first learned to cook this dish, I had no idea what it was but I knew I loved the word. I have always loved words. Their sound, their texture, their flavor. All the sensations that you experience in your mouth that are totally beyond their literal meaning.

When you make shakshuka, you want to use a pan that can move from stovetop to oven. A well seasoned cast iron skillet is perfect. I love seasoning and reseasoning my pans, just as much as I love seasoning in my food. And in my wordplay.

Reseasoning is an obvious but perfect metaphor for "starting over'' without totally abandoning your past. Just like people, cast iron accumulates experience—burnt bits, dry spots, scars from kitchen mishaps. All these moments when we didn't give our skillet enough love or attention. But, you don't need to throw it away! When you reseason, you can slowly slough away all that gunk, and the pan is good!

I love this ritual. It appeals to my love of detail, and my passion for working with my hands. My cast iron pans glisten! So, when I go to start my roux for this creamy green Shakshuka, the sauce swims across the bottom. No sticky bits! Now, I have a cat named Shakshuka, who loves to play with my
other cats, Hoagie and Scrapple. They are also great Shakshu-chefs.

I've now added the recipe to my breakfast repertoire, and I proudly announce to Lauren as she walks through the door: "I've made SHAKSHUKA." And I say the name, savoring all the flavors in the word, the dish, and our spicy, feisty new cat.

WHAT YOU'LL NEED:

1 lb, asparagus
1 lb, spinach
½ onion, diced
2-3 cloves garlic
1 tbsp olive oil
¼ tsp red pepper flakes
salt and pepper
2 tbsp butter

2 tbsp flour
¼ cup of milk
3-4 eggs
½ cup of Parmesan cheese (freshly grated)

crusty bread

WHAT YOU'LL NEED TO DO:

1. Preheat oven to 400°.
2. Prepare your veggies. Dice the onion and garlic. Set aside. On a bias, slice the asparagus so they are decently thin—¼ to ⅛ of an inch.
3. In an oven-ready skillet, saute the ½ onion diced until softened in olive oil. Add the garlic and stir until fragrant. Add your asparagus with a little salt and cook until softened. Remove cooked vegetables from the pan and set aside.
4. Add the butter and melt until foamy. Add in the flour, salt, red pepper flakes, pepper and stir constantly until you have a toasty smelling roux that's the color of peanut butter. Thin it out with a bit of milk and add the cooked asparagus and the spinach. Cook until the spinach has wilted and it's a thickened saucy consistency. Remove from heat.
5. Create four divots in the sauce. Crack eggs into the divots. Cover the whole skillet with Parmesan cheese. Place in oven for 10-15 minutes or until egg whites have firmed up. Serve with crusty bread.

BY FRANNY & CONNOR & AMANDA

Once upon a time, there was a little girl. She had magical powers that made it so cookies could appear wherever she wanted. She even made it so there was a new day of the week where people could only eat cookies. But one day, this little girl didn't want cookies any more. She was tired of cookies. She wanted something more. So, she went on a journey.

She ventured deep into the Big Ice mountain outside of her town. There, she stumbled upon a giant white Ice Cube. But when she got closer, she realized that it wasn't an ice cube at all! It was a giant marshmallow!

"This will be perfect for what I want to make back home" she said. So she pulled a big chunk out of the marshmallow and popped it into her backpack.

But she knew there was still more to be found to make the dish she craved. So, she rafted down the river of chocolate. She stuck her hands in the syrupy deliciousness and pulled out big hunks of milk chocolate. These were the next ingredient for her recipe, and she knew it. She had marshmallows and now chocolate. So what else could she need? While licking chocolate off her fingers, she set off to the desert for the final piece.

Braving a sandstorm of cookie pieces, she arrived at the deserted temple that housed her final ingredient. Legends told that deep within the temple lie a Graham Cracker tablet that would marry perfectly with her marshmallow and chocolate.

But just as she was about to place her hands on the Cracker crust, a large tyrannosaurus rex ambushed her. What was she to do? She thought quickly and blurted out "Cookiecadabra!" Suddenly, within the jaws of the T-Rex appeared a chocolate chip cookie which he crunched right down on. Satisfied with his treat, he curled up and fell asleep. Our little adventurer snuck past the slumbering beast and made off with the Graham Cracker tablet. At last! The final piece of her recipe!

With a backpack full of ingredients, our young hero returned to her town to make her final treat: these S'mores Cookiecadabra Pancakes. She made enough for her mom, her dad, and her younger brother to enjoy. Satisfied, she fell into a deep post-brunch nap so she could prepare for her next big adventure.

WHAT YOU'LL NEED:

box pancake mix
milk or water
chocolate chips or broken up chocolate scraps
marshmallows
butter

WHAT YOU'LL NEED TO DO:

1. Mix pancake mix according to the box directions. Fold in a handful or two of chocolate chips to your mix.
2. Preheat an oven or toaster oven to 200° with a pan in the oven to keep the pancakes warm as you cook them.
3. Heat a large non-stick pan on medium high. Once heated (you can check by dropping some water in the pan and seeing it "dance"), add a tablespoon of butter. Let the butter melt and pour your pancake mixture into the pan.
4. Be prepared for a "first pancake" disaster. It's ok, this is your cooking snack.
5. Flip pancakes once you see small bubbles forming in the batter, and watch out for burning the chocolate. Repeat this process till all the pancakes are cooked up, adding more butter as needed.
6. Once the pancakes are done, cover the pancakes in marshmallows and chocolate chips if desired. Turn the oven on high broil to toast up the marshmallows. Enjoy, forks, optional.

NOTES

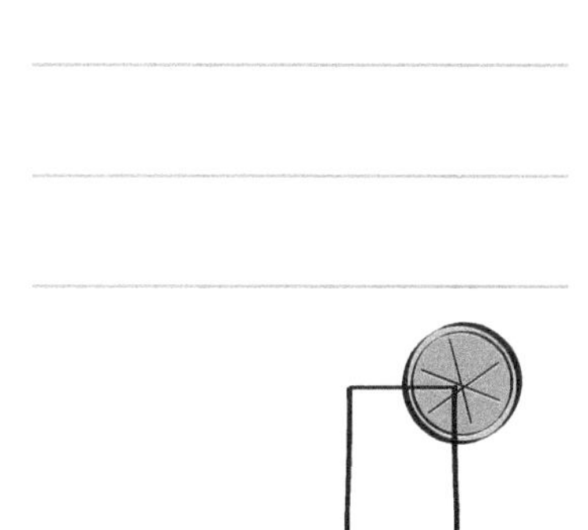

GREAT GRANDMAMMY DAVIS' BACON HUEVOS RANCHEROS

BY FRANNY & CONNOR & KRISTEN & LEX

What does rancheros even mean? As I recently learned, it does not mean to put ranch dressing on your eggs even if you are out of sour cream. You see, I never studied Spanish, or any of the history surrounding this dish, but I can only assume rancheros has something to do with a ranch. A dish one would make while out working the fields, roaming around the desert and living a chill rugged lifestyle. When I met Lex and Kristen and they taught me this version of Huevos Rancheros, I knew I had found the perfect story for this dish without having to do any work on my own.

Lex's great grandfather was a cowboy, living in Montana. But when I say cowboy, it's gilding the lily, which is city folk talk for speaking pretty about something bad. You see, he was a bank robber riding with a horse gang, stealing from trains and banks. They had a secret hideout where they'd stash their ill-gotten gains. When they really got to robbing, they would be out all night. The next morning they would return to their hideout where Great Grandmammy Davis would make this dish for them. Unfortunately, chorizo, the traditional meat for huevos rancheros, was too expensive for them. So Great Grandma Davis used the inexpensive bacon. Famished after their criminal activity, the gang would munch on these huevos rancheros to satisfy their hunger. After they chowed down on Grammy Davis's food, the gang would fall into a sleep that lasted for the rest of the day.

Kristen's family was of a different world. They were more eclectic. They owned a line of saloons, whose signature dish was chorizo baked beans, which was perfect to soak up one of Grandpappy's infamous Saloon Slammers, their signature tequila cocktail.

Now, on their anniversary, Lex and Kristen want to combine their history, and honor both of their Wild Western heritages.

To make this dish, rip off your shirt and work only in your tank top. Cook the onions until they are dead, refry the beans until they melt down to a beautiful buttery gloop. Insist your partner break into the last taco kit so she can have the corn tortilla you know she wants. Top with pine nuts to show how rich you are, and how far you've come from your humble, itinerant criminal beginnings. And eat in an abandoned cave in the mountains with some saloon hooch to remember where you came from.

WHAT YOU'LL NEED:

1 yellow onion, sliced
1 can black beans, 15 oz
¼ cup of water or veggie stock
2 tbsp butter
4 eggs
5 to 6 strips cooked bacon
3 to 4 tortillas, corn or flour, toasted
salsa, avocado, sour cream or pine nuts to garnish

WHAT YOU'LL NEED TO DO:

COOK THE REFRIED BEANS FIRST!

1. Add black beans, and water or stock to a pot. Season with salt, pepper, and cumin if you have it. Bring the pot to a boil and then reduce to a simmer. Cook, stirring occasionally until the beans break down. This will take most of your cook time—around 20 minutes—so keep on eye on it while it simmers away on your back burner.
2. Meanwhile, add the butter to a cast iron skillet and heat on medium low until foamy. Add the onions with salt and cook until golden brown.
3. Crumble up the bacon and set aside.
4. In the cast iron skillet, move the onions around til there are four indentations. If more butter is needed, add it here. Crack the eggs into the holes and cook until desired temperature.
5. Serve the rancheros by spreading a layer of black beans onto a toasted tortilla. Place eggs and onions on top of the tortilla and sprinkle bacon on top of the whole thing. Garnish with salsa, sour cream, avocado, or... if you want.... toasted pine nuts.

GRANDPAPPY'S SALOON SLAMMER

1.5 oz silver tequila
1.5 oz lime juice
1 oz St. Germain
club soda or seltzer

6. Pour the tequila, St. Germain and Lime Juice in a cocktail shaker half filled with ice. Shake to combine.
7. In a chilled glass, add seltzer water and ice. Strain mixture into cocktail glass and serve with a lime or grapefruit wedge.

MAMMA, BUTTA LA PASTA!

Mamma, Butta La Pasta is a famous Italian phrase that every Italian mom wants to hear from their grown son who still lives with her, as he returns home at the end of the day. "Mom, throw the pasta" is so magical, because, in cooking, timing is so important. You can spend all day simmering the sauce, but if you don't time it out exactly, you are stuck with overcooked or cold lumpy noodles. So, traditional Italian cooks get the water boiling before you get there, and throw the pasta in upon your arrival, to ensure this perfect timing. Now, these are hard times, and no one expects you to be the perfect pasta throwing Italian housewife, but a lot can be learned from generations of women who made meals out of almost nothing and relied on the economy and versatility of an ingredient that only that cooks up in the time it takes your loved ones to remove their shoes, wash, and sit down at the table. Or, in our modern case, to clear the coffee table of our WFH setup, open up a bottle of wine, and pull out the pasta plates. Some Italian tricks to take your pasta from good to great: Salt your water to the taste of the sea, reserve some pasta water to thin out your sauce if needed, boil the pasta to the exact timing on the box, and experiment with al dente.

RECIPES!

BY FRANNY & CONNOR & KATE

I love fall but call me basic and I'll cut you down to size like the crisp autumn air slices through the rustling golden leaves of the D.C. Arboretum. It's decorative gourd season y'all, and I'm grabbing up as many pumpkins as I can find. And who doesn't love a cozy cardigan to warm you as you stroll through a fall festival sipping hot apple cider? People can be really judgmental about this season but

I've never understood why. And before you even ask, yes I love pumpkin spiced everything so keep your opinion to yourself. Fall has always felt more like a rebirth to me than the rainy season of Spring.

And it was in fact last fall that I experienced a rebirth in my culinary prowess. After getting lost in a local hay maze, I came upon a tiny squirrel who had been separated from their mother. As I knelt down to examine the situation, he jumped right up onto my shoulder and whispered in my ear, "Please help! I am so hungry! Do you have any butternut squash?"

As luck would have it, I had roasted a whole butternut squash the night before which I turned into a delightfully creamy fall soup. To me, squash screams autumnal bliss. Not one to deny a talking animal, I took the squirrel back to my house where I cooked him this Fall Squash pasta with radiatori. The smells wafting out of my kitchen were incredible. So good, as a matter of fact, that the momma squirrel tracked us down by the scent of my delicious pasta alone. She took a plate, too, and well, now I have a problem. Every Thursday from the months of September to November, a scurry of hungry squirrels arrives at my back door demanding this fall squash dish. Make it for yourself! But, remember, don't feed the squirrels!

WHAT YOU'LL NEED:

½ butternut squash, cubed and roasted (do this with leftovers!)
¼ cup olive oil
salt and pepper
1 red onion
1/2 pound radiatori pasta, ideally smaller with lots of ridges
1 or 2 large cloves garlic, minced
1/2 cup red wine (or white if that's what you have)
1 ounce goat cheese
1 tablespoon chopped fresh sage, if you've got it
Parmesan cheese, to serve

WHAT YOU'LL NEED TO DO:

1. In a large pan, saute onions and garlic in olive oil on medium low until nice and carmelly, as long as you can. At least 15-20 minutes. You will finish the dish in this pan.
2. Salt your pasta water until it "tastes like the sea." Cook the pasta for a few minutes under the time you find on the box. Reserve the pasta water for later.
3. Throw the butternut squash in with the onions and garlic and turn up the heat to medium high until the squash breaks down into a paste. Toss in the wine (red or white, whatever you've got) and reduce.
4. Finish cooking the pasta and then add to the butternut squash sauce. Add reserved pasta water to loosen up the dish if necessary. Top with goat cheese, grated Parmesan (or both) and sage leaves if you've got it. If you've got extra wine, pour yourself a glass and enjoy!

NOTES

SALSICCIA E PAPA

BY FRANNY & CONNOR & SCOTT

When you're improvising in the kitchen, confidence is key. But having family to lend a helping hand is even better. This rustic Italian dish is perfect for a set of two hands—two best friends, a father and a daughter, or whoever you have in your household. Sausages browned by one while another tends to the sauce. Red peppers and roasted broccoli add a splash of color to make sure you're getting a healthy plate of food. Your family of up to four will love it. Just don't go too salty in case your loved ones are sensitive. Make sure you use up all the spices from your encyclopedic library of spices. Let your daughter pick the pasta, she'll thank you for it, and for the fact that you skipped the sardines!

WHAT YOU'LL NEED:

4-5 Italian sausage links
1 can whole red tomatoes (800 grams)
1 red bell pepper, roughly chopped
olive oil
red wine
½ yellow onion
garlic, as much as you like, at least 3 cloves
salt and pepper
oregano (dried or fresh)
red pepper flakes
Italian cheeses like Parmesan, or Pecorino Romano
1 lb hearty pasta of your choice! spaghetti is recommended

BROILED BROCCOLI

1-2 heads of broccoli, cut longways
salt and pepper
olive oil
lemon

WHAT YOU'LL NEED TO DO:

1. At least an hour before, if possible, take your sausage out to get to room temperature. Again, never cook up cold meat. Francesca will get sad.
2. Dice up the garlic and onion. If you are lazy, use our food processor hack on page 25 and blitz it up baby. Set a large pan on low to medium heat. Add 2 tablespoons of olive oil and then your garlic and onion, salt and pepper. Saute it on low low while you collect and prepare your other ingredients.
3. You can either slice up the sausage with skin on, or remove skin and pull out the ground meat. Turn up the heat in the pan, and toss the sausage meat in and let it brown up. (De-glaze with a little red wine if you like.) Add the can of tomatoes and break up the tomatoes in the pan.
4. Adjust heat so it's got a nice simmer going. Keep stirring, making sure the sauce doesn't burn on the bottom. Add some red wine if you've got it, ½-1 cup, a couple dashes of oregano, and salt and pepper as needed. When you've got about 15 minutes left on your simmer time, you can start your pasta pot, filled with water salted like the sea, boiling.
5. While your sauce is simmering and your pasta water is coming to a boil, turn on the broiler on your toaster or convection oven. Line a sheet pan with foil, lay out your broccoli, and drizzle with olive oil, salt and pepper. Add some cloves of garlic if desired—unpeeled for ease. Broil until you get a nice char on them. When they are done, top with squeezed lemon and set aside.
6. Cook the pasta as directed by the box, drain, serve, and top directly with the sauce and grated cheese.

NOTES

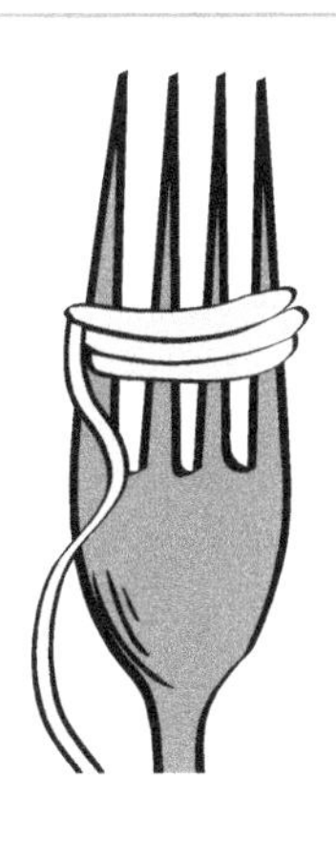

BOLOGNESE A LA JONESESE

BY FRANNY & CONNOR & MEGAN

A large part of reparenting ourselves has to do with balance. Our convenience culture sometimes makes it tempting to get a quick bite out—maybe at Runza or another fast food joint on a long midwestern highway. But sometimes, the best treat is the one we can make ourselves. This veggie packed protein filled pasta dish is good for a cold winter night cuddled up on the couch, a large festive party of friends and even serves well as a reheated microwave lunch. Like the casseroles we all know and love, this easy to throw together pasta dish packs all the flavor and goes great with a simple spinach salad. A heavy dose of red pepper flakes opens up the palette so that you can savor all that rich tomatoey goodness. This is the kind of dish that could take eight hours or eighty minutes but it's sure to come together no matter how much time you have. We recommend a hearty pasta here, but feel free to try with one of your choosing.

WHAT YOU'LL NEED:

BOLOGNESE

1 lb ground beef
1 can whole red tomatoes
(800 grams) (optional)
olive oil
red wine
beef broth (not required)
½ yellow onion
garlic, as much as you like,
at least 3 cloves
1-2 carrots
1 stalk of celery
fresh basil
tomato paste
salt and pepper
red pepper flakes
Italian cheeses
like Parmesan, Pecorino
Romano or mozzarella

Hearty Pasta of your choice!
Spaghetti is recommended

SPINACH SALAD

1 lb fresh, washed spinach
citrus, lemon or lime
salt and pepper
olive oil

WHAT YOU'LL NEED TO DO:

1. At least 1 hours before, if possible, take your ground beef out to get to room temperature. Do not cook cold meat! It will not be happy or delicious!
2. Start with the sauce base, the soffritto or diced onion, garlic, carrots, and celery. If you are lazy, blitz it up a bit in the food processor. Set a big, deep pot, ideally a Dutch oven, on low/medium heat.
3. Add 2 tablespoons of olive oil to the pot and then add your soffritto, salt and pepper. Saute it on low low heat while you collect and prepare your other ingredients.
4. Once the soffritto is nice and soft (be careful not to let it burn), you can raise the heat to medium and add the beef. As it cooks, break it up with your utensil, and let it brown. Add a couple tablespoons of tomato paste.
5. Bolognese is a beast. It can take as long as you want to cook. The more time, the better, but you know your life and how long you can budget for this cook. From here you can go low and slow, or keep the heat up and cook the meat faster. Keep it on as low a simmer as you can, and continue tasting, adjusting the balance of tomato/thickness by adding more tomato paste, or thinning out the sauce with our liquids, the acid by adding more wine, or the savory/fat by adding more beef broth. Keep stirring, making sure the sauce doesn't burn on the bottom.
6. It's your sauce! Experiment with it! You can also make it as tomato-y as you like! If you want a more meat-forward sauce, use only tomato paste. If you want a more tomatoey saucy sauce, add the canned tomatoes in when you've got about 30-40 minutes left on your simmer time, and continue to adjust the levels of tomato paste, wine, and broth. Add more salt and pepper if needed, and those red pepper flakes if you are feeling spicy.
7. At this point you can start your pasta pot, filled with water salted like the sea, boiling. Cook the pasta as directed by the box, drain, serve, and top directly with the bolognese. If you've got leftover sauce, keep it on a low on the stove for awhile longer while you eat!
8. Cheese Check: What do you have? Pecorino, Parmesan, mozzarella? All are welcome here. Garnish with gusto according to your diary (or non-dairy) desires. Tear up from fresh basil on top.
9. Pair this with a refreshing Spinach Salad (or whatever greens you've got handy), dressed simply with lemon, oil, salt, and pepper. If you like, serve the whole thing with a big, bold red wine.

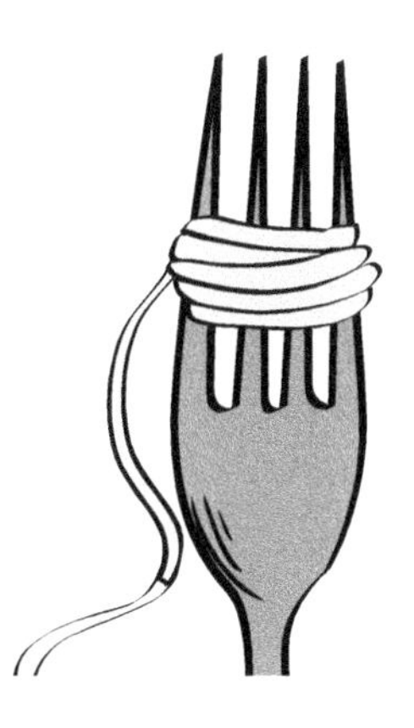

BY FRANNY & CONNOR & NATALIE & MICHAEL

Mushrooms weren't the only thing they were foraging.

Natalie and Michael's families are very food-oriented. Food is about working through shit and being together. They learned this from their great-great grandmothers, Marge and Rita. Natalie's great-great grandma, Marge, was a chicken farmer. Michael's great great-great grandma, Rita, was a mushroom forager. They met in the third class steerage of the Pearl Diver, a ship carrying them to the U.S. from the old country. It was over a breakfast of old crackers and black coffee that they first met and bonded over their mutual love of creamy coffee. They fell in love and dreamed of opening a restaurant together. Through their old European dishes, they could share a bit of their history with their new country and their children. Amidst the cargo on their voyage, they developed a revolutionary chicken and mushroom egg noodle pasta recipe as their flagship dish. But they knew their love was forbidden! Before they parted at the docks, they made love. In their heat of passion, Marge shared all the secrets of poultry to Rita who willingly gave up all her expertise in the art of mushroom foraging. At the end of the night, they each slipped copies of the recipes into the other's boots to serve as a reminder of their true love and their culinary dreams together.

Thirty years later, Natalie and Michael were each foraging in the wild forests of Washington, DC, just like their great-great grandmothers taught them. Engrossed in their foraging, they didn't see each other as they both reached for the same plump shroom. Their hands touched hovering above the fungal parasol. Their eyes met, and it was love. Immediately, Michael and Natalie got to talking about the pasta they were going to make with these mushrooms. Strangely, they both had inherited a very old recipe for mushroom chicken pasta that their family's both stored in an old boot.

The couple felt themselves drawn to each other—as if there was something familiar in the other. As they each pulled out the matching recipes that their great-great grandmothers Marge and Rita wrote, they knew it was fated to be. Their great-great grandmothers not only taught them to forage for mushrooms, they taught them to forage for love. Now, these lovers make their great-great grandmas' recipe for themselves in their Takoma Park apartment that they share with their three beautiful cats. And they make it as creamy as they want.

WHAT YOU'LL NEED:

FOR THE CHICKEN BOOT PASTA

1 lb of boneless chicken thighs
1 lb of cremini mushrooms
½ cup of white onion, diced
1 tbsp of olive oil
2 tbsp of butter
2 tbsp flour
¼ cup heavy cream
1 sprig fresh rosemary
1 lb packet of egg noodles

FOR THE GARLIC LEMON ASPARAGUS

1 lb of asparagus
2 tbs olive oil
3 garlic cloves
1 lemon (we will use the zest and the juice)

WHAT YOU'LL NEED TO DO:

FOR THE CHICKEN BOOT PASTA

1. First, cube the chicken thighs and break apart the mushrooms—removing the stem, peeling the skin and tearing them into bite size pieces. I am a firm believer that you should never put a knife to a mushroom because I believe I heard someone say once that it breaks apart their fiber in a weird way. This ill-broken mushroom fiber results in a terrible texture that puts many folks off our fungal friends. Sprinkle the chicken with salt and pepper. Set aside.
2. Heat a pot of water and cook the egg noodles based on the package's instructions. Salt your pasta water!
3. Next, in a wide deep skillet, heat the oil over medium high heat. Add the onions and cook until translucent. Then add your chicken and saute for 5 minutes, allowing some of its fat to render into the pan. Add your mushrooms and a bit more salt and pepper.
4. Cook until the mushrooms have broken down, and the chicken looks cooked—probably about another 10 minutes. There should be some nice browning at the bottom of the pan. Remove the chicken and the mushroom from the pan and set aside.
5. Reduce the heat to low and add the butter to the pan. Cook till foamy trying to scrape up all the browned bits in the bottom of the pan. Whisk the flour into the butter and cook until you have a mixture that has the texture and color of peanut butter. Next, stir in the heavy cream and break down the mixture until you have a creamy sauce. Here, add the sprig of rosemary, the chicken and mushrooms and mix until combined. Cook until the rosemary is fragrant.
6. Add your cooked pasta to the pan with the sauce and stir to combine. Before serving, remove the sprig of rosemary and enjoy.

TO MAKE THE LEMON GARLIC ASPARAGUS

1. Heat oven to 450°
2. Dice your garlic and cut off the stems of your asparagus. Zest the lemon being careful not to hit the pith. Place your asparagus on a sheet pan lined with parchment paper or aluminum foil. Drizzle with olive oil, dice garlic, salt, pepper, and lemon zest. Then, get in there with your hands to combine it all.
3. Roast in the oven for 10 to 12 minutes. The asparagus should have some charring. Serve with lemon wedges for real lemon fiends.

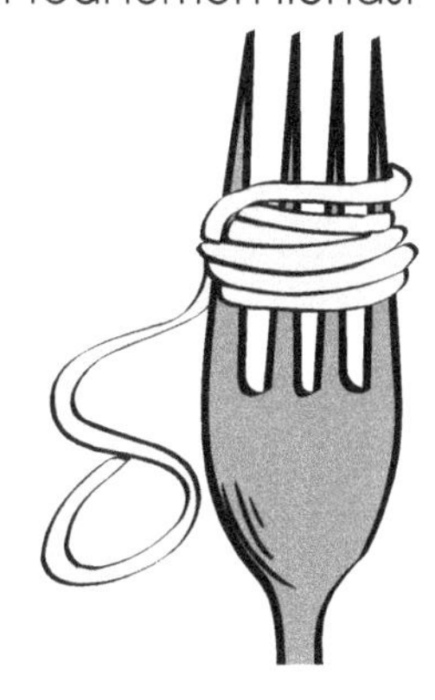

BACK OF THE PANTRY BITES

We all know this feeling. It's been a long day of non-stop zoom calls where no one could find the mute button. Or you're just getting off of a busy shift slinging coffee for folks who make it their personal mission to ruin your day. You get home, kick off your shoes, slump onto the couch and then—your tummy rumbles. With your last remaining ounce of energy, you pull yourself into the kitchen, open the refrigerator, and find that you haven't gone grocery shopping in over a week. You've only got some pantry basics—pasta, rice, garlic, beans, maybe leftover imitation crab meat?

In moments like these, it can be so easy to just pick up your phone and order out. And maybe you really do want that. But, if you're feeling as courageous as some of our audience members in this section, we can show you how to turn those pantry items into a dish that'll knock out that post-work day exhaustion. In this section, you'll find dishes made from pre-made ingredients for those of you who might be running low on what you keep around your kitchen.

One thing that Connor found a bit difficult when he first started cooking was what exactly one should keep in one's pantry. What he's learned after taking a peek into pantries from across the U.S. is that it really depends on how a person cooks. For example, you'll probably find garlic in almost every recipe in this cookbook. That's because Fran and Connor rarely make a dish without it. A couple of guiding principles for picking pantry items:

What kind of flavors do I like to cook with? (Sour? Sweet? Umami?)

What textures do I want in my food? (Crunchy? Smooth? Springy?)

What ingredients do I keep running out of because I use them a lot?

While a whole book could be written about the proper spice cabinet, Connor always likes to have canned anchovies on hand as well as calabrian chili peppers, Parmesan cheese, and garlic. Saute all those together, toss it with some angel hair pasta and there you have dinner in under ten minutes.

We also encourage you to check out pantry items you might not be familiar with and see how they work in your cooking! Miso paste, gochujang, chile de arbol are all used in various cuisines from around the world. Start off with a recipe you want to try and, as you get comfortable with it, experiment! See how it works in other recipes. Before you know it, you'll be a star culinary improviser.

RECIPES!

THE MI-YUMMI HEAT NACHOS

BY FRANNY & CONNOR & MARY & CHRIS

This is not just a story of nachos. This is the journey of nachos. It's a bildungsroman of one man claiming his ability to make nachos the way that one man wants. That man is Lebron James.

The Scene: The night of "The Big Final Game" The Miami Heat vs. LeBron James' team. Backstage, Mr. James is performing his pregame ritual, stretching, meditating, and making nachos with his basketball colleagues—or "teammates" as we're told they're called.

Most food stories are about bringing people together; this is about one man standing apart, against soggy nachos. All his life, LeBron has been told how to live his life: how to play and how to eat nachos. All his life, LeBron has been playing basketball the way that HE wants. But, alas, he has NOT been eating NACHOS the way he wants.

His fellow "teammates"—on the team(?) that he plays for(?)—always put every ingredient upon the tortilla chips, drowning the poor delicate corn babies, who congeal and wilt in the oven. They never had a chance. A soggy, claggy mess that tortured LeBron to no end. It was a team beef that started infecting more than their nachos. It was interfering with his game, and tonight was THE BIG GAME. He needed to COOK the Miami Heat.

So for once, in the locker room kitchenette of the place where they do basketball, LeBron finds himself alone. Everyone else must be warming up. Idiots. He looks around. He takes a breath. He looks up. A single bead of sweat blossoms from his forehead, and journeys down the side of his face, splashing onto the pan of tortilla chips. The sweat covers a single chip. He lifts the chip up, regarding it. He nibbles it. Still crunchy. For now. And then it comes to him: put the wet ingredients AFTER you pull the nachos out of the oven.

And so he did, strategically covering his tortilla chips with cheddar cheese and, for the first time, savory CHICKEN! He baked those cheesy corn babies up all crunchy. Then, he sprinkled his hot sauce on top. He sniffed it. He tasted it. He'd done it. The perfect, cheesy, spicy, crispy nachos. The perfect pregame meal.

And then, as he entered the basketball playing field. He spied us in our usual, front-of-the-court side seats and smiled. He recognized us, obviously. He winked at us, and jogged over.

"Good times and ready to roll!" Lebron James said, and then, pulled something out of his athletic pants's pocket, discreetly pressing a cheesy piece of paper into our open, hungry hands.

AND THIS IS THAT RECIPE

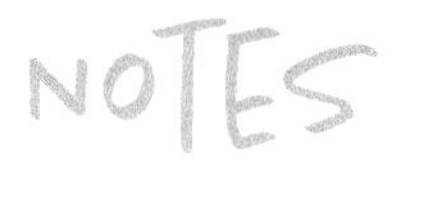

WHAT YOU'LL NEED:

1 lb chicken breast, cubed
1 bag, tortilla chips
2 cups, grated cheddar cheese
1 ½ tbsp neutral cooking oil
1 tsp ground cinnamon
2 tbs hot sauce (Tabasco or Cholula is fine here)
salt and pepper

WHAT YOU'LL NEED TO DO:

1. Preheat oven to 400°.
2. Cut chicken into cubes and place in a bowl. Add the salt, pepper and ground cinnamon to the bowl and mix with your hands or tongs. Set aside.
3. Heat a medium size pan—cast iron preferred—over medium heat. Add oil and cook chicken through. Set aside. This can be done ahead of time.
4. After the chicken is cooked, grate the cheese or get it out of the bag. Arrange the tortilla chips on a cookie sheet covered in aluminum foil. Layer one half of tortilla chips on the cookie sheet and sprinkle with half the cheese and half the cooked chicken. Repeat with leftover ingredients.
5. Place the nachos in the preheated oven for 6-8 minutes or until the cheese has melted through. Top with hot sauce.

PEPPY CHIHUAHUA'S RUSTIC FAJITA QUESADILLA

BY FRANNY & CONNOR & COLIN

When I was but a wee child, my father would make incredible Mexican food to nourish me after a long day at school. Watching him toss veggies and proteins in a cast iron pan, it made me want to take up cooking myself. I was so desirous of la comida Mexicana that I went to Oaxaca and came home with my own Mexican chihuahua. We named him Peppy. This dish is in honor of him.

Fajita Veggies, chicken breast and smoky cumin combine to give the taste of the food my father cooked me. I added my own spin with a non-traditional BBQ sauce topping. I pour it over the quesadilla like a Dunkin' latte to create a sweet and smoky sensation that reminds you that life isn't always about being perfect. In fact, sometimes we need to get a bit messy to relive those after-school moments that brought us joy.

WHAT YOU'LL NEED:

2 tortillas
1 chicken breast
½ tsp cumin
1 red bell pepper, sliced
½ yellow onion, sliced
2 garlic cloves, sliced
BBQ sauce*
¼ cup cheddar cheese, shredded
(Colin used cheddar slices, here)
salt and pepper
juice of a lime

WHAT YOU'LL NEED TO DO:

*These are Colin's fajitas, and Colin loves BBQ sauce. If you don't, feel free to omit the BBQ sauce. It's your life and it's your fajitas!

1. Slice the garlic and onions longways, to create nice little circles of garlic and rings of onion. Cut the bell pepper into long strips, as wide as you like.
2. Mix up in a bowl with salt, pepper, cumin, and any other spices you've got (chili pepper, paprika, etc.), and a little bit of neutral oil (canola, grape seed, etc.).
3. Pat down your chicken breast with paper towels, then season with salt, pepper, cumin, and your spices.
4. Heat a large pan on medium high. Once at heat, add 1 to 2 tablespoons of neutral oil and get a nice sear on the chicken breast. Continue sautéing until chicken is cooked thoroughly—4 to 5 minutes. Pull chicken out and let cool for about 5 minutes, until you are able to slice up or shred with forks.
5. Keep the pan on the heat, and add more oil if necessary, and fry up your vegetables.
6. Assemble the quesadilla for toasting: Two tortillas, cheese, your chicken and your vegetables (cover in a squeeze of lime). Cook 'til the cheese is melted and toasty—quesadillas are intuitive. Flip when necessary.
7. Serve covered in more cheese and/or BBQ sauce.

NOTES

NOTHING IS REAL/ NOTHING MATTERS: ANNIE'S SPECIAL CRAB MAC AND CHEESE

BY FRANNY & CONNOR & BROOKE & SAM

Mr. Sam was a sad man. He had lived a difficult life. First, his house burnt down. Then, his wife left him, and, while she was walking out that door, she was eaten by a crocodile. Tragically, this mirrored the death of his only daughter, Annie, who was eaten by a whale. With nothing left to live for, Mr. Sam vowed two vows. First, he vowed reveng against all aquatic life. So, he moved to a lake and decided to rid his new home of all swimming things. This also helped him fulfill his second vow—to never have his house burn down again. (Since it would be so close to the water that you can like splash the water over to the house.)

On this lake, Mr. Sam lived a simple revenge-filled life. Each day was exactly the same. He wakes up at 4am, drinks his cup of coffee, and eats a fried egg. He puts on a gray sweater and a gray hat and goes outside into the foggy weather. He boards his boat, the "Mr. Truman," and hunts his fishy prey—the object of his revenge.

But one day, something was different. A cute little crab hopped out of the lake and scurried up his fishing pole. Startled, Mr. Sam looked down at the crab who was looking deep into his eyes, almost like a human. Then, the crab spoke: "Mr. Sam, this is NOT real. You are in an imitation boat in an imitation lake full of imitation fish. Even I, your only conduit to the outside world, am an imitation crab."

Mr. Sam lost it! He took his fish gutting knife and stabbed the imitation crab in between the eyes. After he murdered the crab, he knew he had to remove all trace of the conversing crustacean. When he made his normal dinner of Annie's Mac and Cheese, (his daughter's special recipe), he put in chunks of the imitation crab.

Eat the imitation crab. Add the American cheese and brie cheese. This is reality. You are not in a simulation. Go crazy, nothing matters. Thank you for listening to NPR WHYY 90.9. Become a monthly donor if you can.

WHAT YOU'LL NEED:

1 box Annie's Mac and Cheese (White with shells preferred, but any instant mac and cheese works here)
2 tbs milk or heavy whipping cream
1 cup imitation crab meat
½ cup panko bread crumbs
½ cup grated Parmesan cheese
¼ cup brie cheese
salt and pepper

WHAT YOU'LL NEED TO DO:

1. Fill a pot with water and salt it til it tastes like the sea. Add the noodles from the instant mac and cheese. Follow the instructions on the box that call for milk and boil pasta one minute less than required.
2. Meanwhile, add the panko bread crumbs and Parmesan cheese to a dry skillet. Toast til crumb is golden and Parmesan is fragrant.
3. Drain the pasta and reserve 1 cup of the pasta water (just in case). Return pasta to pot.
4. Add milk, brie, black pepper, crab meat, and instant mac and cheese flavor packet. Stir until combined. Add additional pasta water if mixture is too thick.
5. Serve in bowls and sprinkle toasted parm crumbs on top.

BODEGA "POKE" BOWLS

BY FRANNY & CONNOR & SAMUEL & RAMON

Samuel and Ramon are experts in making things beautiful. They can look at simple things, and find the natural beauty and transform it into something high fashion. For example, Ramon can sculpt a gorgeous fresh octopus which Samuel will turn into a headdress for a photo shoot. Even with the pandemic, they have filled their eyes and their bellies with beautiful things. They spent most of the pandemic in Mexico City, eating the best food in the world. But, even with the abundance of fresh, quality ingredients, they still craved some of the diverse options they left back in New York City. The craving at the top of their list was sushi.

When Samuel and Ramon left New York City in October 2020, they did not know where they were going to live but they knew they were going to be together. That was what was important. As their city apartment stood vacant, time stopped in the empty space but also it didn't stop. Signs of their absence were scattered about like the mail that daily fell through the slot in their apartment door. When they finally returned, vaccinated and healthy in May 2021, they had to wade through a pile of letters, bills and promotional material sent to them over many months. Their kitchen, of course, was empty, so their first stop for food was sushi, and to stock up on smoked salmon and simple snacks to nourish them from their long day of international travel.

Always down to get creative, they turned their bodega booty into Japanese-inspired marinated salmon, leftover toast points, cheese and apples with honey. They built these snacks with all the love and creativity that has filled their twenty years together. Twenty years of fun they'd never know before they met. They shared this improvised meal in celebration of their ten year wedding anniversary,
and Ramon's birthday. They look forward to reviving their life together, full of beauty, creativity, health, and hope.

WHAT YOU'LL NEED

1 packet smoked salmon
1 takeout seaweed salad
1 takeout of sushi (1-2 rolls per person you're feeding)
2 apples
4 slices white bread
6 mini baby bell cheeses
¼ cup honey

Note: All of these were purchased from a bodega shortly before the performance

NOTES

WHAT YOU'LL NEED TO DO:

1. Deconstruct your takeout sushi, placing rice in one bowl, and everything else in another bowl.
2. Cube bread, cheese and apples to a similar size. Toast the bread in a dry skillet until brown on all sides, and place it in a bowl.
3. Add apples and cheese. Drizzle the whole thing with honey.
4. Layer smoked salmon and seaweed salad on top of your sushi rice, Sprinkle any extra goodness from the sushi on top.
5. Enjoy both bowls side by side.

BY FRANNY & CONNOR & CHRISTINE & MICHAEL

I grew up working in a kitchen. My mom's friend ran a restaurant called "Lindsey's Culinary Kitchen," and, as soon as I legally could, I started working there. For my whole life, I have always loved food and cooking. And I'm good at it too. It has been an incredible superpower to have, and has served me both professionally and personally. In fact, my cooking ability came in handy during a pivotal moment in my life. You see, it quite literally saved me from falling overboard and into the Chicago river.

At the time, I was living in the Windy City, and it was my 24th birthday. My friends flew in for the weekend, which was a big deal, because I hadn't seen them since I moved out here. We had a whole big weekend planned. I was going to take them out on Saturday, and—SURPRISE—my friends booked a booze cruise for Sunday morning at 10:00 AM. Now, I am a person who loves logistics, planning, and problem solving. Usually food is somehow the answer. I knew that we would never make it on that boat that early if we didn't have something to line our stomachs after our Saturday night. That's why, on Friday, I made like five pounds of vegetable fried rice.

Saturday night was amazing! So amazing that I woke up on Sunday still drunk. I stumbled to my fridge, pulled out the Tupperware of fried rice, sat on my kitchen floor, and ate it with my hands. Covered in oil and full of vegetables and starch, I felt like a superhero. As we made our way to the booze cruise, however, I started to sober up, and could feel my superpowers being sapped by my only kryptonite—a wicked hangover. I felt rough. NEVER get on a boat to sober up! That being said, I was not like my friends, who hadn't scarfed down handfuls of rice on the kitchen floor, and I did NOT barf off the side of the boat at the first sign of choppy water.

This dish became a staple throughout the partying of my twenties. I remember it fueling many more nights of debauchery. This fried rice still brings so much comfort to my soul and to my belly. It is so simple. Cut up the vegetables, fry the rice, throw in an egg. Throw a crab in there if you like. (Especially if you are on a boat.)

I can't party as hard anymore, but I love teaching my Booze Cruise Vegetable Fried Rice to my elementary students at the culinary institute. But, because they are too young for hangovers, I call it "Christine's Special Party Rice For Your Tummy." And this is that recipe.

WHAT YOU'LL NEED:

1 red pepper, diced
½ onion, diced
2-3 garlic cloves, diced
½ tsp, ginger paste
½ cup green beans, chopped (frozen is fine)
½ cup broccoli florets, quartered (frozen is fine)
1 ½ cups, cooked white rice
2 eggs
1 tbsp neutral oil
1 tbsp soy sauce
½ tsp sesame oil

WHAT YOU'LL NEED TO DO:

1. Prep vegetables. Dice red pepper, onion and garlic. Chop green beans and broccoli florets into bite size pieces. Set all veggies aside. If using frozen, let them thaw slightly on the counter before putting into a skillet.
2. Heat oil in a skillet over medium high heat. Add onion and saute until it's softened. Then add your red pepper and stir to combine. Finally, add your garlic and ginger paste.
3. Saute until the pan is quite dry and you're building up some browning on the bottom of your pan. Add soy sauce to de-glaze the pan. To this, add your green vegetables and saute until they're bright green and fragrant. Add your cooked rice and stir to combine. Finally, add your sesame oil and sesame seeds (if you have them).
4. Into the hot rice vegetable mixture, crack two eggs and stir until it makes a custardy and fluffy consistency. Serve immediately. Garnish with sesame seeds.

THE GLAMOROUS ROASTED RED PEPPER LENTIL BEEF TIP COCONUT CURRY

BY FRANNY & CONNOR & RACHEL

My kitchen is a battlefield.
This recipe is bloody.
This recipe is dangerous.
This recipe is a revolution.
This recipe is a cure.

When you hear "Glamorous and Powerful Roasted Red Lentil Beef Tip Coconut Curry," it might just sound like a warm, nourishing comfort dish perfect for an unexpectedly cold April night. Well, you'd be wrong because it is so much more. This dish is a powerful weapon against the pain of many people's existence: the yeast infection.

Rachel developed this dish after she finally sought the advice of a naturalist for a yeast infection that traditional medicine could not resolve. Her naturalist said that she has an overgrowth of candida spread through her whole body. Her treatment became culinary. She had to starve and kill the candida within her. Her kitchen became the site of a raging war between her and the deadly host that had taken up residence inside her.

Now, Rachel loves food, and has spent her life learning different techniques to feed herself in a way that was pleasant to her. Now, thanks to all her culinary combat, she can give herself this glamour gift: she can make herself something delicious. But, how did she starve the candida while still feeding herself? Well, dear reader, this recipe is the answer and the cure.

No sugars or yeasts to feed the candida, only glorious fresh flavorful food. To make this dish, she smashed the garlic the way that Marcella Hazan taught her. She burnt the red pepper in effigy and slashed the onion with the sharp knife given to her by a friend. She split the lentil with her bare hands. The result: a gorgeous spiced ruby red and turmeric yellow curry that vanquished her candida, as well as her appetite for food that brings her joy.

Her kitchen is a battlefield.
This recipe is a curse.
And this recipe is the cure.

WHAT YOU'LL NEED:

½ lb leftover beef tip
1 cup red lentils
1 cup coconut milk
1 cup broth (veggie or chicken)
½ yellow onion, diced
2 garlic cloves
1 red bell pepper
1 tbsp tomato paste
2 tsp turmeric
1 tsp curry powder
½ tsp cumin
½ tsp cinnamon
1 tbsp neutral oil
couscous for serving

NOTES

WHAT YOU'LL NEED TO DO:

1. Heat 1 tbsp of oil in a deep skillet over medium heat.
2. Add onions, turmeric, curry powder, cumin, and cinnamon. Saute till onions are translucent.
3. Saute garlic until fragrant. Add tomato paste and cook until everything is a deep red.
4. Add lentils and stir into mix. Add coconut milk and broth. Bring to a boil and reduce to a simmer. Let simmer uncovered til lentils begin to break down. About 20 minutes. If it starts to look dry, add more broth.
5. While lentils are cooking, roast red pepper over a gas stove flame until it's black all over. Let cool in a paper bag.
6. Use this time to cook couscous based on the packaging instructions
7. Once red pepper is cooled, wash off any black. Cut off the stem and de-seed. Dice the roasted red pepper and salt to taste.
8. The lentils, at this point, should have broken down completely. Stir in leftover beef tip and red pepper. Serve over couscous.

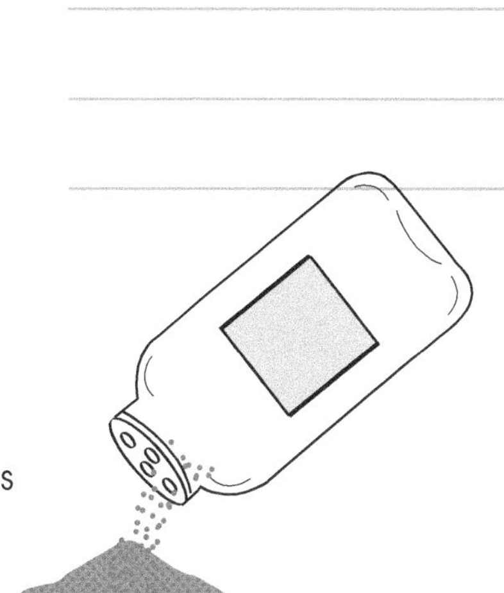

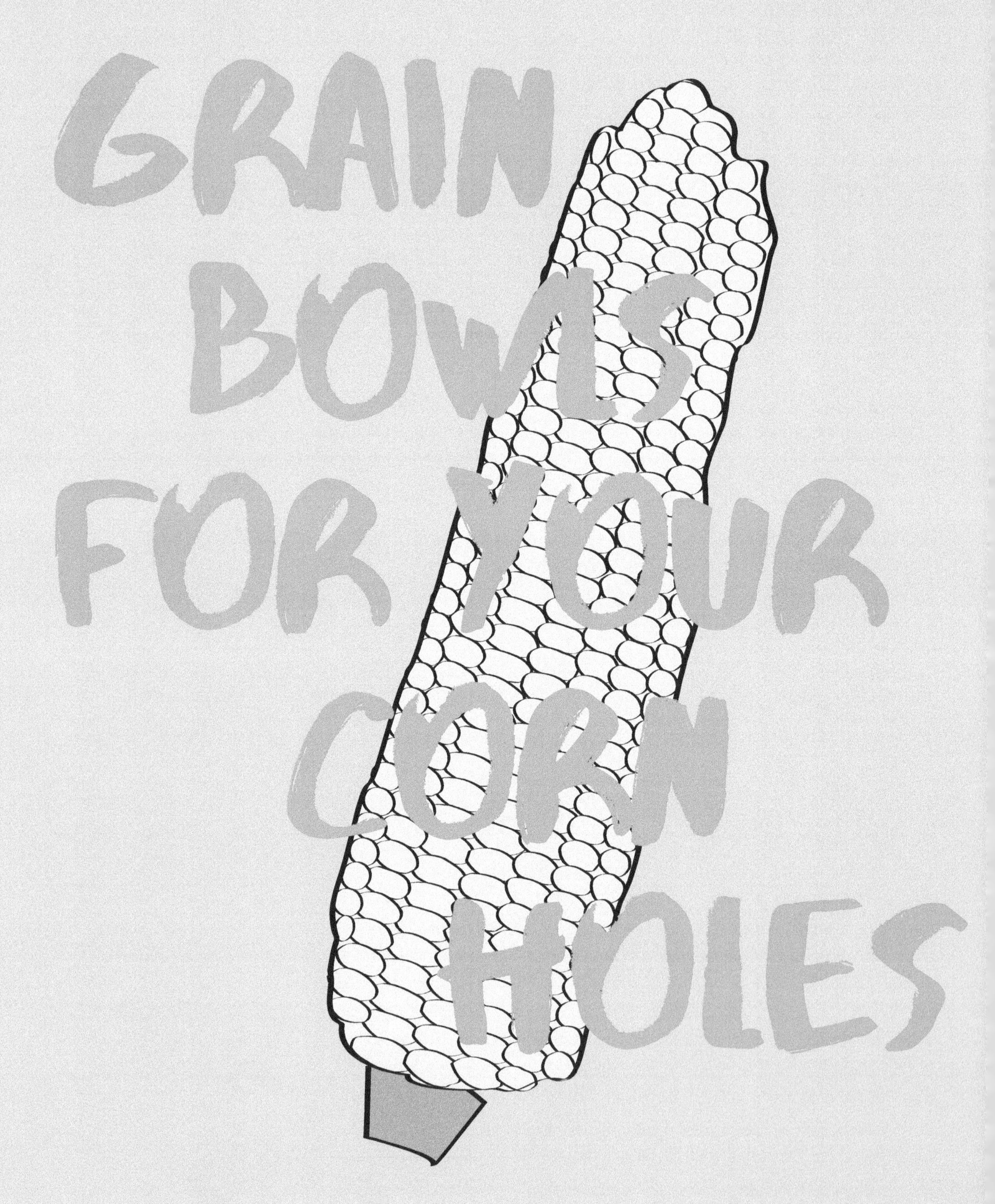
GRAIN
BOWLS
FOR YOUR
CORN
HOLES

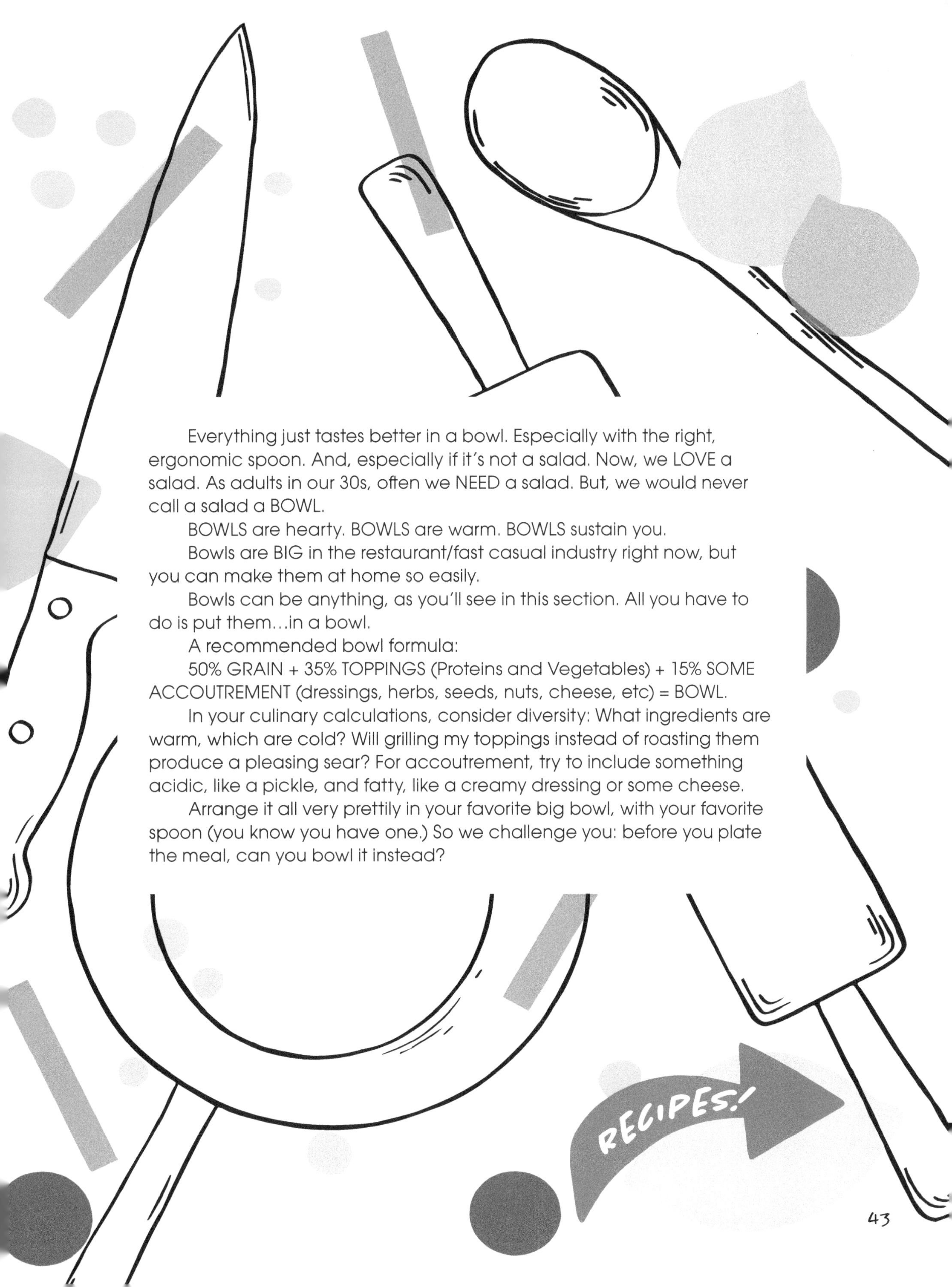

Everything just tastes better in a bowl. Especially with the right, ergonomic spoon. And, especially if it's not a salad. Now, we LOVE a salad. As adults in our 30s, often we NEED a salad. But, we would never call a salad a BOWL.

BOWLS are hearty. BOWLS are warm. BOWLS sustain you.

Bowls are BIG in the restaurant/fast casual industry right now, but you can make them at home so easily.

Bowls can be anything, as you'll see in this section. All you have to do is put them…in a bowl.

A recommended bowl formula:

50% GRAIN + 35% TOPPINGS (Proteins and Vegetables) + 15% SOME ACCOUTREMENT (dressings, herbs, seeds, nuts, cheese, etc) = BOWL.

In your culinary calculations, consider diversity: What ingredients are warm, which are cold? Will grilling my toppings instead of roasting them produce a pleasing sear? For accoutrement, try to include something acidic, like a pickle, and fatty, like a creamy dressing or some cheese.

Arrange it all very prettily in your favorite big bowl, with your favorite spoon (you know you have one.) So we challenge you: before you plate the meal, can you bowl it instead?

Disappearing Cold Noodle Dish

BY FRANNY & CONNOR & BRETT & DENISE

When Denise was growing up in New York City, she experienced many different types of cuisine. Hopping from one amazing restaurant to the next with her dear friends, she began to notice that her palate had become very refined. To this day, she continues to experiment with flavors in the kitchen. Unfortunately, she had yet to crack the elusive recipe she once ate at a Japanese restaurant: the cold King Oyster Mushroom Yaki Soba noodle.

It was when she was thirteen years old that she last tasted this dish. Denise's friend took her to the most amazing little noodle shop, guiding her by the hand through many twists and turns of Chinatown. There, they shared the most amazing Yaki Soba with King Oyster Mushrooms. She was so excited to take her family back, but when she returned to the street where she tasted this dish, the restaurant was gone! For the rest of her youth, she wandered Chinatown searching for the shop but to no avail.

From then on, she pursued challenging puzzles and riddles, hoping to keep her mind sharp and powerful. She hoped that, with all this practice, she could finally solve the great puzzle that was the location of that magical restaurant. As an adult, she would often be found working through puzzles—even at parties. It was at one very fateful party, where Brett first approached Denise as she was working on a particularly challenging nautical themed puzzle. Peering over her shoulder, he could see the exact spot that Denise was missing. In a swift movement, he placed a small goldfish into the empty space in the puzzle. Denise looked up, their eyes met and the rest, as they say, was history.

Brett proved to be a brilliant and supportive partner to Denise. He would help her with any problem she might have—whether they were based in fantasy, like getting out of an escape room, or rooted in reality, like all the challenges she conquered when she first taught remotely. Yet, in all their time together, Denise was still haunted by the specter of the uncrackable Cold Yaki Soba noodle dish. Oh, what sweet irony!

One prematurely hot May day, Denise put aside her lesson plans for planting sunflowers with her kindergartners to make dinner. She was so full of hope, thinking about being back in person, with all those babies and baby sunflowers. So full of hope that, as she looked into the fridge for dinner inspiration, an ancient knowledge descended upon her like a metric ton of squid falling right on her head. She called out "Brett, come quick! I've solved the cold noodle recipe puzzle. It's been inside me the whole time!" For the rest of the evening, they cooked and laughed, these two seekers of challenge and love brought together in the game board of life with a little goldfish of hope in between them. And, with one metaphor slapped together with another, the goldfish is, somehow, this recipe.

WHAT YOU'LL NEED:

2 scallions sliced
1 bundle of soba noodles
2 garlic cloves, diced
1 lb of oyster, shitake or maitake mushrooms
2 tbsp soy sauce
1 tsp sesame oil
1 tsp chili oil
½ tsp fish sauce
1 tsp of gochujang
1 tsp of rice wine vinegar
sesame seeds for garnish

WHAT YOU'LL NEED TO DO:

1. Prepare the mushrooms by brushing off any dirt and tearing them apart with your hands to manageable pieces. They should be about bite size. Try to refrain from using your knife. Make sure you prep all your ingredients before you put your wok on. This will all go quickly!
2. To a wok, add neutral oil until it shimmers. Add mushrooms, garlic and salt and pepper. Cook til mushrooms are done.
3. Put a pot of water on to boil and prepare to make the soba noodles
4. While you wait for the water to boil, add all the sauces to a small boil and whisk together. Add any extra seasoning (salt or pepper) you desire.
5. Boil soba noodles according to cooking instructions on the package. Remove once they are cooked, strain and run cold water to stop the cooking process.
6. Plate the noodles, add the mushrooms on top, sprinkle with sliced scallions, sesame seeds and pour the dipping sauce over the whole dish. Eat cold.

Note: This could also be served warm by adding the noodles to the wok.

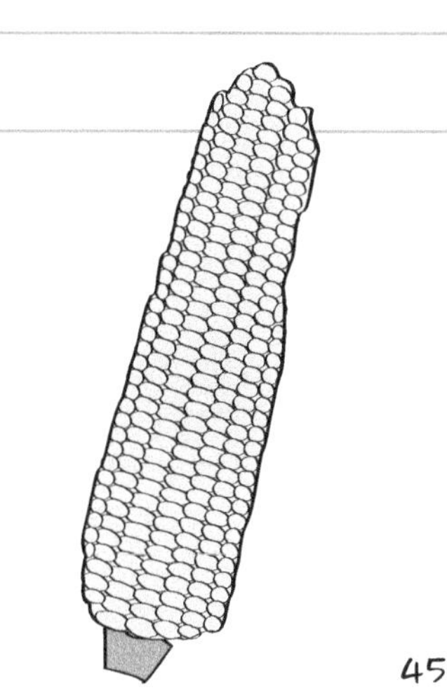

BY FRANNY & CONNOR & CLAIRE

Claire loves to win. She has had more jobs than Jesus Christ who famously had only two—carpenter and being our Lord and savior. By sixteen, she was a backup figure skater for the Olympics. At twenty, she was an acclaimed actress and model. And now, she's a well-respected pastry chef who dominates the kitchen. Claire loves winning.

But what does a girl boss do when she needs a girl break? She calls up her friend Alexis to have a relaxing day in the park with her friend's new baby girl, Fiona. Together, these three women let their hair down in Malcolm X Park for a day of no responsibilities and plenty of wine.

Rosé is a mandatory at these meetings (Fiona has juice), and they all indulge in some refreshing lady time to fuel them for their next week of conquering the world. They feast on this decadent and healthy grain bowl. Mushrooms for protein, asparagus for fiber and feta cheese for... well cheese. On top of it all, a delicious fattoush salad with fresh tomatoes and cucumbers. Sated and satisfied, they watch the sun go down.

It's hard to keep your competitive edge without rest. Claire knows this. She's a pro at napping too. So when you've had it up to here, take a break with Claire's Girl Boss Grain and Gab Farro Bowl. Oh, and make sure you have a friend to gab with too.

WHAT YOU'LL NEED:

1 cup farro
1 lb mushrooms washed, dried, and sliced in half)
1 lb asparagus washed and trimmed)
1 red onion or shallot
1 lemon
2 tbsp red wine vinegar
2 tbsp olive oil
½ cup feta cheese
fresh tomatoes and cucumbers
any fresh or dried Mediterranean spices you've got
(parsley, oregano, basil, red pepper flakes etc.)

NOTES

WHAT YOU'LL NEED TO DO:

1. Cook your farro according to the package instructions, making sure to salt your boiling water. Once complete, set aside in a big bowl, and toss with a glug of olive oil.
2. Toss the asparagus and mushrooms in a bowl with olive oil, salt/pepper, and any dried spices you are using. Grill up asparagus and mushrooms.* Once nice and charred, squeeze with lemon and set aside.
3. Dice up the tomatoes and cucumbers and your onion (or shallot). Set the onion in a small bowl with salt, pepper, and 2 tablespoons of red wine vinegar—or enough to cover the onions.
4. Mix the tomatoes and cucumbers in a medium bowl with some lemon juice, olive oil, and salt. Let et macerate, giving it a stir every once in a while.
5. When you serve, toss the shallots in the tomato/cucumber salad, with some of the leftover vinegar to taste, and toss with any fresh herbs you've got on hand.
6. Plate! A scoop of farro topped with grilled vegetables and your fattoush salad on the side. Cover in as much feta cheese as you like!

*If you don't have a grill or grill pan, you can roast up the veg at 425° F. Makes plenty of leftovers, and will be really good cold tomorrow. Store components individually, or toss together.

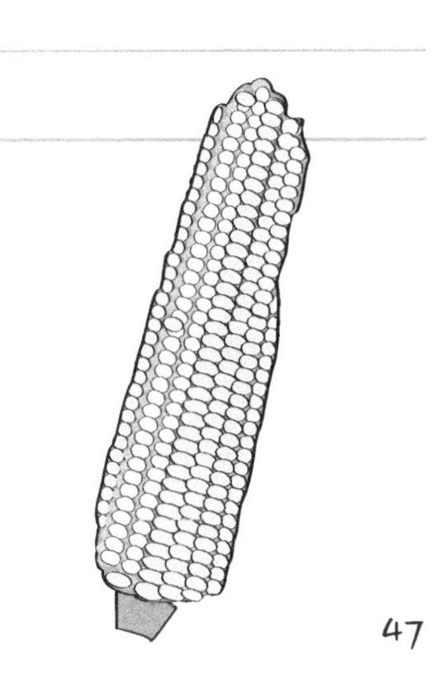

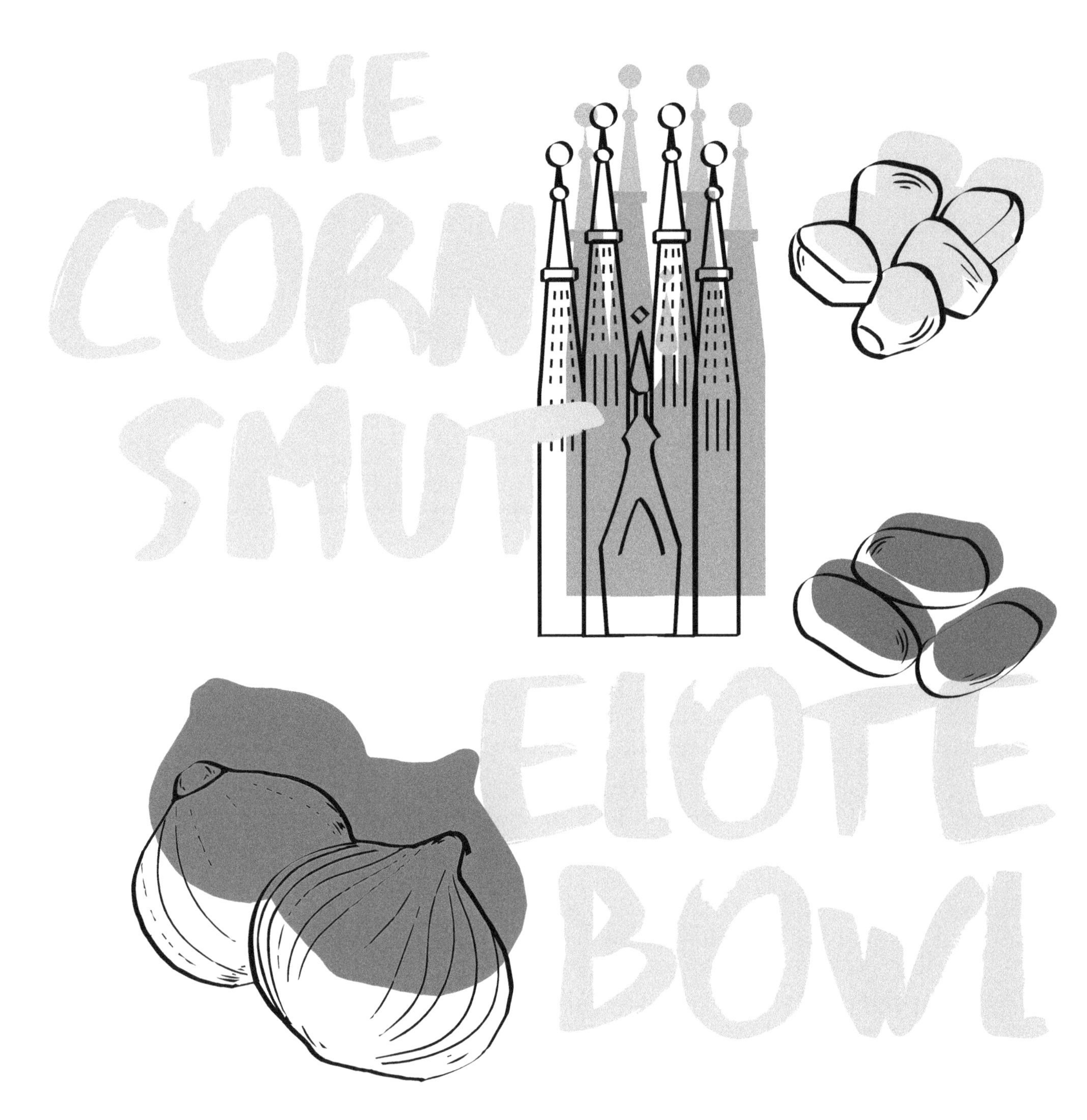

BY FRANNY & CONNOR & DIVA BABY

Why does one ever go to Barcelona? To find themselves in the beauty of the Iberian Peninsula or to lose themselves in the architecture of Gaudí? When Diva Baby and Corn Smut, best drag friends, headed to the beautiful city, they were open to anything. Diva had been recently booked in the hottest gay club in downtown Barcelona, Pasaido del Mar or "Not the Bottom You Were Thinking Of." After a performance that could only be described as shake-the-house-down-boots, Diva Baby caught the scent of something. The luscious creamy and smoky scent drove them wild.

"What is that smell?" they said to their friend Corn Smut.

"Elote, Baby!" Corn Smut said "You can get it on the street!"

But Diva was too busy to leave the club and head out to a street vendor. They were simply having too much fun. After a raucous night of partying, however, Diva was kept awake all night by the alluring scent of corn. The next morning, they stomped downstairs, and took a big gulp of coffee from a pot that was made by their AirBNB host, Truck, a non-binary Mexican ex-pat living in Barcelona.

"How'd you sleep?" Truck asked.

"Oh, I couldn't get any rest," Diva replied breathlessly. "I kept dreaming about elote!"

"I can make you that, Diva!" and Truck set right to work.

Even though elote is traditionally a Mexican dish, and shouldn't be found in Barcelona, Truck knew how to adapt a recipe developed by their abuela. They adapted the dish based on the ingredients that they had on hand: canned corn, black beans, cheeze, mayonnaise and even more cheese.

Diva stood transfixed at this culinary tango. They memorized it so they could eat it whenever they liked. Topped with a quick pickle of red onions and a soft boiled egg, this Elote Corn Bowl makes a perfect brunch and conjures up the memory of those steamy Spanish nights we all long for.

WHAT YOU'LL NEED:

1 15 oz can of corn
1 15 oz can of black beans
2 to 3 garlic cloves, minced
1 tsp cumin
½ red onion, sliced thin
¼ cup of white vinegar
juice of ½ lime
½ cup of chopped cilantro

SAUCE

¼-½ cup of mayo
¼ tsp ancho red pepper
¼ tsp chili pepper
1/4 tsp smoked paprika
juice of ½ lime
Parmesan and sharp cheddar

WHAT YOU'LL NEED TO DO:

1. Place sliced red onions in a bowl, and salt them. Cover with white vinegar, and lime juice. Set aside.
2. Heat neutral oil in a skillet over medium high heat. Drain the can of corn, and saute. Add garlic and cumin. If you'd like, add more cumin to your taste. Once several kernels are browned up, add the black beans as well and combine.
3. In a big bowl, combine mayo, ancho red pepper, chili pepper, smoked paprika and lime juice. Mix up the sauce, and adjust with more mayo, lime, or spices until it tastes good to you.
4. Mix up the browned corn/bean mixture with as much creamy sauce as desired. Top with pickled red onion, more lime, and cilantro.

NOTES

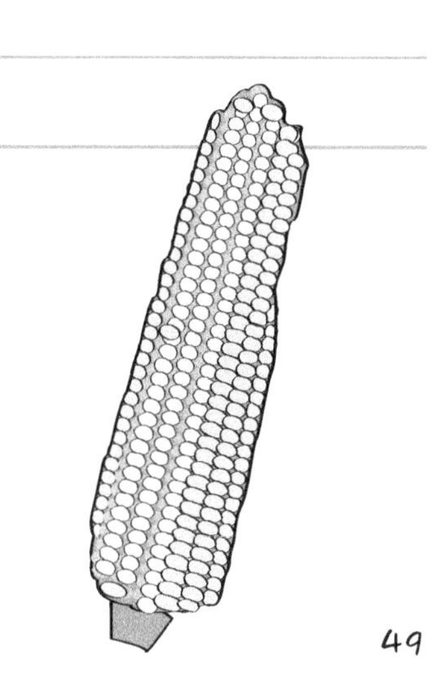

DOOR TO DOOR COMMUNITY BUILDING CHICKEN MUSHROOM PEPPER STIR FRY

BY FRANNY & CONNOR & KAREN

I first met Karen on a picnic in a park in Paris. In a rather embarrassing moment, I had thought her baguette was my baguette, and I had taken a big bite out of it. You can't really blame me, though. Her baguette was like four feet long or like, some amount of meters. It was so long that it reached past her picnic blanket and landed right in my unpasteurized chevre. I was mortified. Little did I know that I not only committed a faux pas, as they say in French, but I had also broken an antiquated French Jaques Pepin Law of 1885. The gendarme was called, but Karen graciously intervened, demanding that no charges were to be filed. Her husband Perry got me off with a slap on the wrist. They used a stale baguette to give me the slap which actually hurt quite a bit.

Karen was magnanimous throughout the whole experience. At the cafe later that day, while sipping espresso and nibbling pan au chocolat, she comforted me by explaining that her deep love of French food—her love of all food—was born when she stole ingredients from the people around her. She told me this story:

"Times were hard growing up in New Hampshire. Things were bland. Lots of boiled food. I like boiled food, but like only once a year on St Patrick's day. You get tired of the only season being salt, and the only cooking mechanism being boiling water.

"One day, I had enough, I decided to explore, went door to door, asking for exciting ingredients and made them give them to me. People had ginger, cumin, fresh herbs (I though they only came dried!), mustard seed! I made them all give them to me and promised to credit them as I used them.

"With my arms full of unfamiliar ingredients, I bounded back home where I whipped up an interesting—yet delicious—spicy veggie heavy chicken stir fry. My family was confused, but eagerly scarfed down the dish. You know, they used to say to me: 'We thought you might be an alien, but we brought you home from the hospital anyways!' From then on, it was my job to cook, but they preferred I get my ingredients in a more traditional way. I was barred from going door to door and instead went grocery aisle to grocery aisle. But, I standby my gathering instincts! It was very community building!

As we watched the sun set behind the Champs Elysse, Karen taught me about stir frying ginger, garlic, pepper, and chicken, ingredients stolen with only the best of intentions, cooked with love.

And this is that recipe!

WHAT YOU'LL NEED:

1 lb of chicken thighs, cut into cubes and salted
1 lb of cremini mushrooms, torn into pieces
1 red bell pepper, diced
1 inch of ginger, peeled and minced
4 cloves of garlic, minced
1 teaspoon of sesame oil
1 tbsp cornstarch
1 tbsp of soy sauce
½ teaspoon of fish sauce
neutral oil

NOTES

WHAT YOU'LL NEED TO DO:

1. This cook is going to be fast! Proper mise en place (which is French for putting everything in little bowls) is essential! Before you even touch a burner dial, make sure everything is diced up and ready to be cooked.
2. As part of your prep, whisk together soy sauce, sesame oil, and fish sauce. Set this aside.
3. Okay, here we go! Heat 1 to 2 tablespoons of neutral oil in a wok or a large skillet over medium high heat.
4. Add red bell pepper and cremini mushrooms. If using a wok, stir constantly. Throw in a pinch of salt and let the mushrooms and pepper release their liquid and soften.
5. Next, add garlic and ginger and saute until fragrant. Thirty seconds. Try not to burn the garlic.
6. Once garlic and ginger are fragrant, add chicken thighs and constantly stir until cooked through. Add the soy sauce mixture and let it coat the veggies and chicken.
7. While the chicken is cooking, whisk together cornstarch with 1/4 cup of water until dissolved. Add cornstarch slurry to stir fry and cook until the sauce has thickened. Serve over white or brown rice.

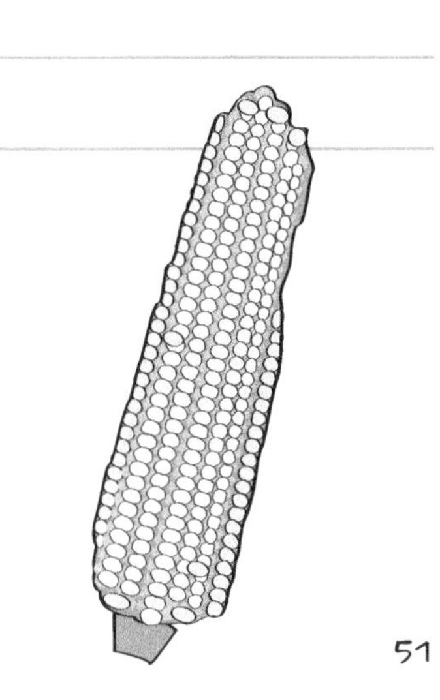

MOLTO COMFY,

MOLTO CLASSICO!

If you don't know, molto means very in Italian. For example, in Italianoglish, a language fluently spoken by Francesca and passably by Connor, the phrase "these sweatpants are molto comfy and I love to wear them while I eat my molto delicioso chicken parmesan!"

Sometimes, a dish can make you feel like the warm comforting hug of sweatpants around your waist. And sometimes a dish is best enjoyed in those warm and comfy sweatpants. The recipes you'll find in this section live somewhere in the venn diagram of these two sensations. Stews and casseroles and (Connor's favorite) chicken Parmesan. Who doesn't love something that's been cooked long and slow? Maybe, you make these recipes when it's cold outside and you want to feel like a winter witch who whips up filling and delectable meals. Regardless of what you're wearing or who you're pretending to be, these recipes can stand in for a weeknight dinner or be an all-day-show-stopping cook for a dinner party centerpiece. No matter what, though, prepare for leftovers—you're going to have leftovers.

Here's the best thing about the leftovers from these recipes: they're sometimes better than when you made them fresh. As delicious as they are, leftovers can be anxiety inducing! Before you know it, your fridge is full of Tupperwares, mason jars, and old leftover takeout quarts containing various roasts and stews and bakes. Peering into the skyline of leftovers in your fridge, getting takeout just seems easier. How do you know what's good and what's not? Connor has tried to keep on top of this by setting aside a couple of hours on every Sunday afternoon to do a fridge inventory. What's still good? What's about to go? And what's a fermented thing that will probably never go bad? By sticking to these three rules, he's able to plan out his weekly lunch menu and also get in some much needed fridge cleaning. Hey, you could even do this while your cioppino is simmering!

Fridge space maintenance might seem daunting at first, but once you have a better understanding of what's in your kitchen at any given time, you're able to whip up meals that shape your family cooking practice.

RECIPES!

MARLENE'S CHICKEN PARM

BY FRANNY & CONNOR & MARLENE

Chicken Parm is the kind of thing you might see on a restaurant menu, but always be too intimidated to cook at home. But, if we sit quietly at our kitchen table, close our eyes, and listen very closely, we can hear the voice of our inner Italian grandma whispering *mangia* to us. We can hear her south Philly accent imploring us to put in *just a handful of this hun*. She is our guide who enchants us with *moozerell*, and implores us to *cook it how ya grandpa likes*. This Chicken Parm recipe is dedicated to her—may she always guide our oven-mitted hand.

This recipe is a simple dish, easy to make for a family of seven or just for yourself at home. The hardest part is keeping your hands clean while you're breading it. Perfect for a side of pasta or to go right into a hoagie if you're feeling midday peckish. With the first bite, you'll be instantly transported back to those warm Philly Sundays when you'd sneak out to the Italian market to gorge on a plate of spaghetti doused in gravy. Feel free to mix up the spices in the breading to suit your tastes. It's always fun to mix it up.

WHAT YOU'LL NEED:

chicken cutlets
flour
Italian breadcrumbs
salt and pepper
1-2 eggs
1 jar of tomato sauce
mozzarella, shredded or torn up

WHAT YOU'LL NEED TO DO:

1. At least one hour before, take your chicken out of the fridge and let it get to room temperature. Never cook cold meat!
2. Dry your cutlets with a paper towel, salt and pepper. This can be done the night before for best results. If the cutlets are quite thick, you can slice them longways to create a thinner cutlet shaped like a heart.
3. Prepare three bowls for your breading: one with flour, one with whisked egg, and one with breadcrumbs.
4. Preheat the oven to 400°. Line a sheet pan with parchment paper. These can be fried in oil, but I prefer oven baked for a healthier, and easier meal! If you like, you can spray or spread cooking oil onto the parchment paper for a fry effect.
5. Bread the cutlets: Dredge in flour, then dip in egg (shake off extra flour and egg before moving on), then coat with breadcrumbs, push the breadcrumbs into the meat with your fingers for staying power. Move breaded cutlets to the prepared sheet pan.
6. Fully bake the cutlets until the internal temperature is 165° F, or for about 15 minutes, flipping halfway through cook. Pull out the sheet pan and spoon the tomato sauce on top of each cutlet, and top with as much mozzarella as you like. Put pan back into oven and continue to heat until sauce is hot and cheese is melted. If you want a little toast on the cheese, you can put the oven on broil.

NOTES

NANA MARY HELEN'S FAJITA RICE RECIPE

BY FRANNY & CONNOR & DEBI

By the time Michael was 12, he was TIRED of chicken. As a good Italian boy, he had eaten chicken in as many ways as the Italians could come up with. Chicken cutlets, chicken Parmesan, chicken piccata, chicken Marsala, chicken et cetera. One day, while at his Nana Mary Helen's house, he revolted against the chicken cutlet. Michael's mother, Debi, was at a loss. She sighed at her son's temper tantrum. How could they make little Mikey fall in love with the chicken all over again. Debi always secretly loved Mexican food, but never felt like she could serve it to her mother. But this was her opportunity! Sometimes children are a great excuse to undermine your parents.

For the first time in her young life, Debi took control of her mother's kitchen. She sent Mary Helen OUT! She went deep diving into her mother's spice cabinet, and struck gold. Mary Helen had purchased a pre-packaged spice collection, filled with non-Italian flavors she had never opened: Chili pepper, cumin, paprika! She rounded out the flavors with some boops of onion powder and garlic salt. Would Mary Helen eat this Mexican inspired fajita dish? Yes! For diabolical Debi covered the whole thing in instant rice, cheddar cheese and let it get all crispy in the oven.

Mary Helen and Michael both were VERY happy with the results! And Michael never complained about uninspired chicken again. Mary Helen demanded to learn this spicy Tex Mex dish, and Debi proudly taught her. These days, Michael doesn't eat chicken at all, but whenever he comes home to Cleveland, his Nana makes her special spicy rice chicken cheddar cheese casserole. Michael tries
not to show his excitement but he always is. When the oozy cheesy, spicy pan comes out, Mary Helen and Debi take their first tastes, and little Michael is always sneaking up behind them stealing his own covert bites of chicken. All three generations take a deep sigh of satisfaction.

WHAT YOU'LL NEED:

1 onion, sliced
1 garlic clove, diced
1 chicken breast or thigh, sliced into strips
1 tsp of garlic powder
1 tsp of taco seasoning
1 packet of instant one minute rice
½ cup of shredded cheese
salt and pepper

WHAT YOU'LL NEED TO DO:

1. Add neutral oil to an oven proof pan. Add onions and saute until translucent. Preheat the oven to 350°.
2. Before adding chicken to the pan, sprinkle salt, pepper, garlic powder and taco seasoning on the chicken. Make space for the chicken and begin to cook.
3. Prepare One Minute Rice as directed by the package.
4. Once the chicken is cooked through, add the cooked rice and saute briefly.
5. Take the pan off heat and cover it with cheese. Place in oven until cheese has melted.
6. Serve with salsa, sour cream, guacamole or warm tortillas.

FLORENTINE CIOPPINO OR THE FLU'S WORST ENEMY

BY FRANNY & CONNOR & LIZ & FRANK

In 1976, Frank and Liz were gallivanting around Europe in matrimonial bliss. They wore out their Europass traveling from Frankfurt to Vienna to Florence. But it was on the Apennine Peninsula that their journey was brought to an abrupt halt. A flu in Florence wrecked Liz's plans and confined her hostel bed–coughing endlessly.

Frank, not to be deterred, set out into the Italian city to find a cure for his new bride. As he wandered down the alleys and cobbled pathways, an old nun beckoned Frank into her Abbey. Nuns shuffled back and forth as they set up an art show. Through broken French and Italian, Frank was suddenly conscripted into being a curator for these abbesses. He hung frames, set up lighting, and swept floors.

After he finished his long day of work, Frank went to track down his new holy bosses only to let them know he had completed his ablutions. Losing himself in the winding halls of their grounds, he came across their commissary where he discovered the nuns slurping down some cioppino–a tomatoey fish stew full of spices and herbs.

For his day's work, the nuns sloshed two portions of the elixir into jars for him to take back to his bride. He immediately headed back to the hostel where Liz was laying on her back with a fever of one hundred and two. But after a few tastes of the holy broth, Liz began to feel the color come back to her cheeks. The spicy red pepper flake paired with the fresh parsley and the tender fish ran through her sinuses flushing out any trace of sickness.

Frank and Liz cook this veggie forward seafood stew to this day. It's a colorful and flavorful dish that reminds them of their time abroad, even when the world feels a thousand miles away. It's perfect with herbs from your own garden, or you can omit them. Serve it with lemon and feel your fever melt away into a Mediterranean mariner bliss.

WHAT YOU'LL NEED:

4 to 5 garlic cloves
1 cup wine (red or white)
1 onion (yellow or white)
10 scallops
20 oz canned whole tomatoes
1 to 2 cod filets (or other whitefish)
3 tbsp tomato paste
½ tsp red chili or red pepper flakes
2 tbsp fresh oregano
(1 tsp of dried if substituting)
2 bay leaves
1 tbsp fresh thyme
(1 tsp of dried if substituting)
½ cup fresh parsley, chopped
(2 tsp of dried if substituting)
1 lemon

WHAT YOU'LL NEED TO DO:

1. Other seafood are welcome in this recipe! Use shrimp, mussels, clams whatever you got! Avoid meaty fishes like tuna or swordfish however.
2. Heat a big pot or Dutch oven on medium low. Once up to heat, add 2 tablespoons of olive oil.
3. Mince up your onions, garlic, and chili (adding only as much as you'd like), and add to the pot to saute.
4. Once soft, add about 2 tablespoons of oregano and 1 tablespoon of thyme and cook up. Add 3 tablespoons of tomato paste. Cook until the tomato paste has browned.
5. Open the can of tomatoes and break up the tomatoes with your hands, blitz through a food processor or use an immersion blender. Pat cod and scallops dry with paper towels. Cut cod into small, bite-sized chunks. Salt and pepper your seafood.
6. Add wine and 1 bay leaf to the tomato paste mixture. Bring the pot to a low simmer and then add the can of broken up tomatoes. Fill the can up a third with water, and add to the pot. Let simmer on low for 15-25 minutes.
7. Taste and adjust the mixture with tomato paste, wine, salt or pepper. When the stew tastes good to you, add the seafood and allow to cook in the stew. Use tongs to pull the seafood out as it finishes cooking and turns translucent.
8. Top with fresh parsley, arugula, squeeze of lemon, and drizzle of finishing oil. Serve with crusty bread.

SPICE
OF LIFE
CHILI
A RECIPE
FOR AND FROM
HARD TIMES OR
SOMETIMES YOU
HAVE TO COME HOME
FOR SOMETHING
DIFFERENT
ANTACID

BY FRANNY & CONNOR & JOEY

I was born in Richmond but I don't really remember it. It's because I moved to Northern Virginia when I was one and a half years old. My parents were just fine cooks, but they weren't very adventurous. So, the first time I went to the Hard Times Cafe tucked away in Manassas, Virginia, my mind and my body was not prepared for the culinary adventure that awaited there.

They had a chili sampler of 4 different kinds. My mouth was overwhelmed with the dynamic flavors and regional styles. How could one dish taste so different? Afterwards, my butthole was overwhelmed. I have not shit like that in my life. Well, at least, not since the infamous Italian Mozzarella incident. But, this night of terror did not diminish my love for chili, and my appetite for all the spices of life! Just like the four different regional varieties of chili in that Hard Times sampler, I have held four different jobs in four different cities in my adult life.

I never want to be stuck doing the same thing. I am holding myself accountable from sameness. So, when the pandemic hit, I moved back to Richmond to be close to the people I loved—without even telling my work. A lot of my friends live here, and many of them work in the restaurant industry. One night, when Tim was working late, and I was throwing up all day, I made him this chili so he would have something nourishing and spicy. Just like me.

WHAT YOU'LL NEED:

1 red onion
1 chipotle in adobo sauce, diced with sauce
3 garlic cloves, diced
1 tsp of cayenne pepper
1 bay leaf
1 tsp of cumin
1 tbsp of tomato paste
1 large can of diced tomatoes
1 lb of ground beef
1 cup of bold red wine
1 can of kidney beans or red beans, rinsed

Add extra chili powder, throw in a bay leaf last minute to see if it makes a difference.

NOTES

WHAT YOU'LL NEED TO DO:

1. To a large pot or Dutch oven, add olive oil and heat on medium high to a shimmer. Add the red onion, chipotle, garlic, cayenne and cumin. Heat til onions begin to break down and spices bloom. Add tomato paste and cook til browned.
2. Add the ground beef and cook until browned, and the tomato onion mixture is incorporated.
3. De-glaze the pot with the cup of red wine. Stir and allow to reduce slightly. Pour in the red beans.
4. To the pot, add the canned tomatoes with their juice. Bring to a boil, add bay leaf and then reduce the heat to low so it's simmering. Let the pot simmer until the mixture has reduced to a thick texture. If it gets to dry, add water or stock.

VEGGIE TIME

Becoming an adult is learning how to like vegetables. And, in this sense...I am fully an adult.

I recently had bad stomach issues, having moved back from Italy. I was eating American food again after 3 years, and my tummy was like, nooooooo. I looked like I was pregnant. I was about to get married. Not a good look. I went to a nutritionist, who cut EVERYTHING out of my diet except for vegetables and lean meats. It was…boring, but it was healing. It was then that I learned to love the vegetable. They become my medicine. I still reach for kale for hangovers like I reached for Advil in ye old days. My husband now packs his own arugula to shove into his Wawa breakfast sammies. We've become…leaf monsters.

You too can improve your vegetable love life! No more soggy spinach! To be in a long term relationship with the vegetable, one needs to learn how to make them taste delicious. It's ALL about how you cook and season them.

Toss your veggies in flavor before you cook them, and cook them well. Salt and pepper them. If you wanna get spicy, add some red pepper flakes. Get some fun seasoning mixes like za'atar. Drizzle with olive oil and top with garlic, garlic, and more garlic.

Get 'em hot! Roast a red pepper over the open flame, grill on high heat. If you don't have a grill, we highly recommend investing in a grill pan.

Finish with squeezes of lemon or lime, or a creamy dressing. Choose your own vegetable adventure!

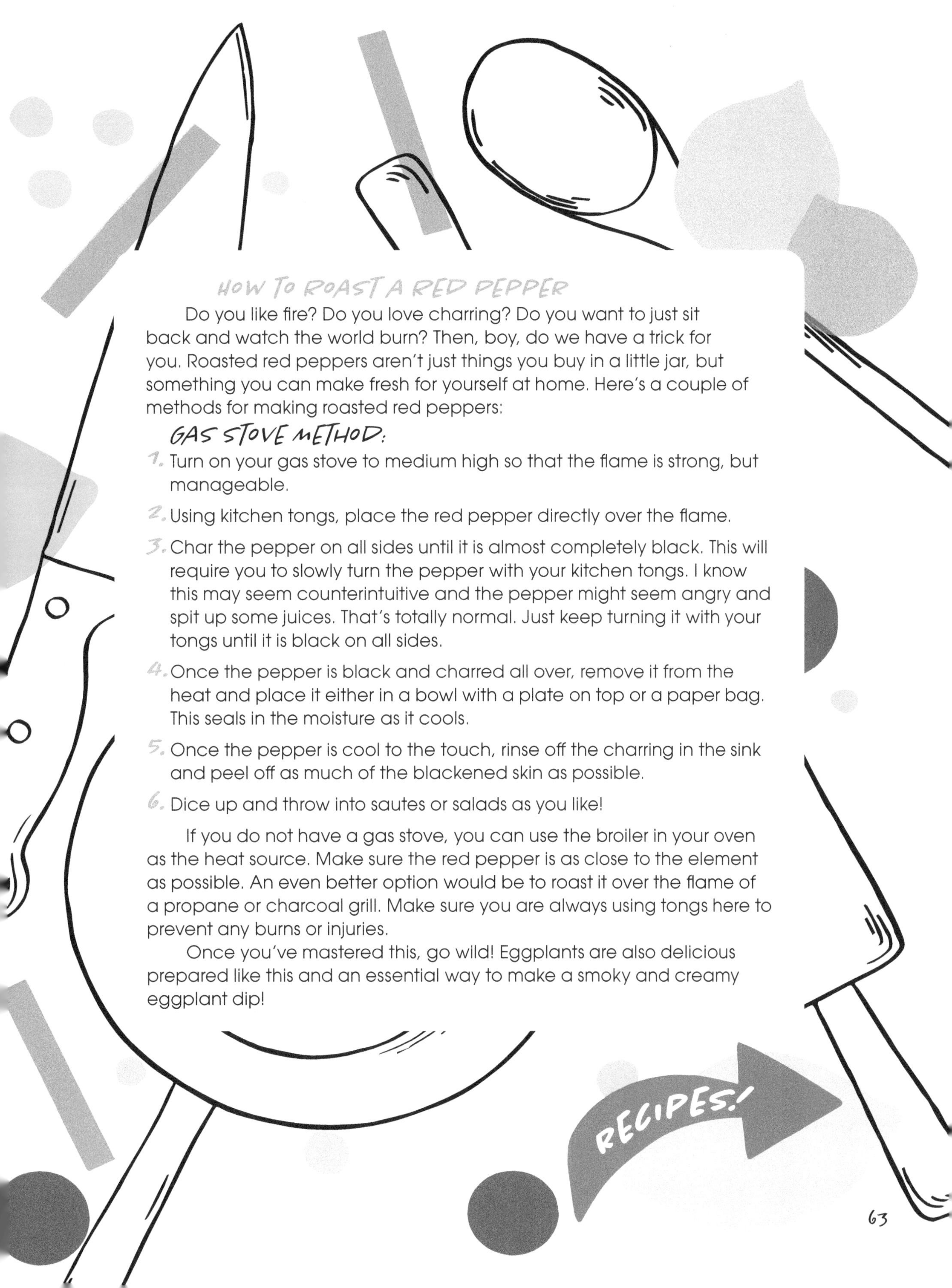

HOW TO ROAST A RED PEPPER

Do you like fire? Do you love charring? Do you want to just sit back and watch the world burn? Then, boy, do we have a trick for you. Roasted red peppers aren't just things you buy in a little jar, but something you can make fresh for yourself at home. Here's a couple of methods for making roasted red peppers:

GAS STOVE METHOD:

1. Turn on your gas stove to medium high so that the flame is strong, but manageable.
2. Using kitchen tongs, place the red pepper directly over the flame.
3. Char the pepper on all sides until it is almost completely black. This will require you to slowly turn the pepper with your kitchen tongs. I know this may seem counterintuitive and the pepper might seem angry and spit up some juices. That's totally normal. Just keep turning it with your tongs until it is black on all sides.
4. Once the pepper is black and charred all over, remove it from the heat and place it either in a bowl with a plate on top or a paper bag. This seals in the moisture as it cools.
5. Once the pepper is cool to the touch, rinse off the charring in the sink and peel off as much of the blackened skin as possible.
6. Dice up and throw into sautes or salads as you like!

If you do not have a gas stove, you can use the broiler in your oven as the heat source. Make sure the red pepper is as close to the element as possible. An even better option would be to roast it over the flame of a propane or charcoal grill. Make sure you are always using tongs here to prevent any burns or injuries.

Once you've mastered this, go wild! Eggplants are also delicious prepared like this and an essential way to make a smoky and creamy eggplant dip!

SUMMER TIME SADNESS DETOX SALAD

BY FRANNY & CONNOR & JACQUELINE & GRAYSON

It has been so cold for so long. All we have for company is each other and Noodles. We have a cat named Noodles, by the way, but, now that you mention it, we also have been eating a lot of noodles. Related, who can say?

I'm standing in the kitchen, drinking Yards Lager Beer, and I turn the oven on to stay warm. As the warmth seeps into my bones, I'm thinking of summer, of fresh tomatoes, of sun on my face. Vitamin D, camping with my family, making pita pizzas on the fire. Bean, rice, and corn.

Summer was simple. It's time to detox and go back to easier times. While noodles are easy, so is this salad. It's got kale and it's got carrots. It feels like summer. It's family, it's fun. It's all going to be ok!

Zazz it up with some pine nuts!!!!

WHAT YOU'LL NEED:

1 bunch of kale
juice of 1 lemon
2 carrots
1 onion or shallot
1 lb mushrooms
3 garlic cloves
1 tbsp pine nuts
½ tsp dried rosemary
salt and pepper
olive oil
apple cider vinegar

NOTES

WHAT YOU'LL NEED TO DO:

1. Squeeze lemon juice, olive oil and a little salt onto kale in a big bowl. Massage the mixture into the kale and rip into bite size pieces with your hand. Get rid of the stalk. Set kale aside to rest for 10 minutes.
2. Slice the carrots along the bias and very thin. In a separate bowl, salt the carrots, add olive oil, vinegar and pepper. Set aside.
3. Dice up your onion (or shallot) and garlic. De-stem and peel the white skin off the mushrooms. Tear the mushrooms into a bowl.
4. Heat olive oil in a skillet over medium. When oil is hot, add the onion and garlic and saute until aromatic. Add mushrooms and cook. Once mushrooms begin to soften, add salt, pepper and rosemary. Continue cooking until everything is brown and caramelized—about 8-10 minutes.
5. In a separate dry pan, toast pine nuts until they are fragrant and brown.
6. Now it's time to assemble the salad. Add the carrots and toasted pine nuts to the kale and mix. Extra salt may be needed at this moment but feel it out. Put salad in bowls for eating, spoon mushroom mixture on top and enjoy!

SINGLE FLAME FALAFEL OR NOT A GOOD DAY TO BE A CHICKPEA

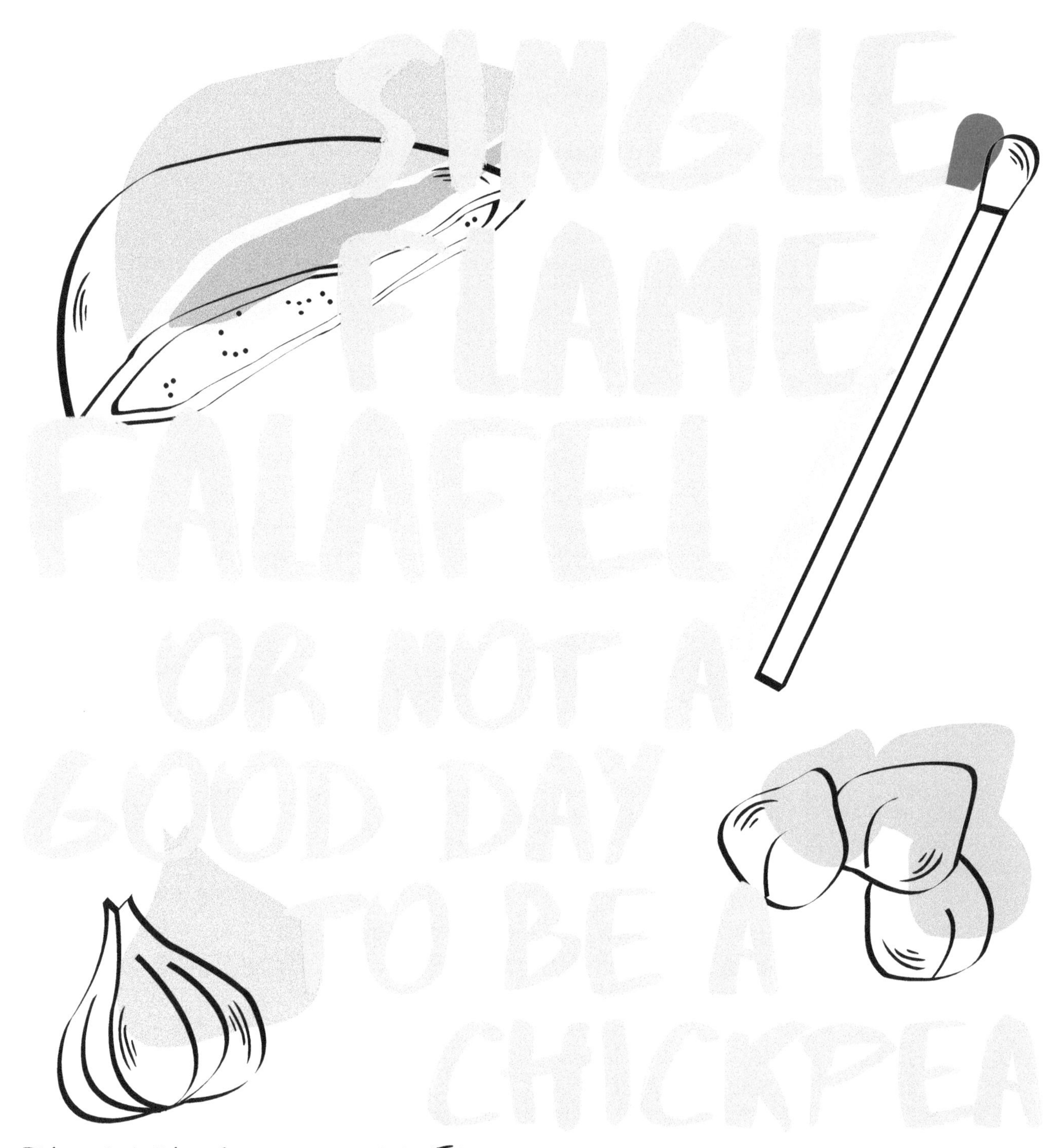

BY FRANNY & CONNOR & JACINTA

I am famous for my bad luck. In the past year our hot water heater broke, we found mold in our kitchen, got in a car accident, my nephew stabbed me in my eye, my vaccine appointment was canceled, and then when I went to a new vaccine appointment, my hubcap was stolen. 2020 was tough. So, for 2021, we have eschewed all normal domestic life. We moved into a tent in our garden, and began a more simple and idyllic life in our Philadelphia backyard.

One morning, while working in my herb garden, a beautiful delicate bird landed on my shoulder. He started to eat my hair!

"No birdie, my hair is not food." I said.

"My name is Bruce." the bird replied "And how I crave for something Mediterranean!" Bruce replied.

Ever the hostess, I thought for a moment and said "My garden is overflowing with parsley and I've got chickpeas on."

"I have irritable bowel syndrome," Bruce yelled, and flew away.

"I love chickpeas," I said to myself. "Why don't I make falafel just for me?"

So, I dove into my tent and handcrafted individual falafel. Because of our hermetic lifestyle, we no longer had an oven. So I cooked it over my only stick with fire. They were so good! So good, in fact, that I opened up a shop called "Single Flame," which only serves what you can cook over a stick on fire. Then, that was too expensive, and with COVID destroying the restaurant industry, we pivoted to a direct to consumer module. We'd send subscription boxes to customers with a one stick, one match, and a recipe.

Give us your credit card number and we'll send you three free weeks of boxes. Share your special code with a friend and we'll give them three free weeks of boxes. Then they'll get a special code to share with their friends and --Oh no!, we've given away too many free boxes.

Author's Note: Single Flame Subscription boxes are no longer in business, we recommend trying this recipe at home with your own stick and match.

WHAT YOU'LL NEED:

1 cup of chickpeas (soaked and cooked. canned is fine!)
4 cloves of garlic, diced finely or grated
½ yellow or red onion, diced
½ cup of parsley, diced
¼ cup of olive oil (plus maybe more)
½ teaspoon of cumin
½ teaspoon of red pepper flakes
salt and pepper
pita bread and tzatziki sauce to serve

WHAT YOU'LL NEED TO DO:

1. Preheat your oven to 375°.
2. Place chickpeas, garlic, onion, parsley, cumin, red pepper flakes, salt and pepper into the food processor. Pulse two to three times til the mixture takes the texture of breadcrumbs.
3. Continue pulsing and add the olive oil slowly. It should start to come together into something that looks mold-able.
4. Using an ice cream scoop or a spoon, scoop even portions (about 1 ½ inches in diameter) onto a baking sheet lined with parchment paper. Dipping your hands in water, roll the falafel balls around to make them more spherical.
5. Bake in a 375° oven for 20 minutes, flipping halfway through. While baking, prepare sides such as tzatziki sauce, olive, and toasted pita bread.

BY FRANNY & CONNOR & SARAH

Today was challenging. I spent the day subject to certain energies from specific energy sources that were not positive energies. When I got home, I was totally zapped. I was starved physically and spiritually. I sought refuge in my kitchen, looking for a snack to nourish me, and to replenish my reserves as a human, a mother, a wife, an artist, and educator! Woof! On my way to raid Jessie's candy bucket, my toe caught against a floorboard and I fell to the floor. I rarely trip, as I am a Lecoq trained mover. Something is amiss, I thought. Dusting myself off, I looked at the floor, and pried away the floorboard.

"I'll have to get the contractor in." My husband is a Realtor and has a ton of great connections. He found this beautiful, historic home in the Germantown neighborhood of Philadelphia for us, which has been so amazing to have through this pandemic. Which is why this loose floorboard was so baffling. Curious to see what's underneath, I continued to lift the board. Underneath was another panel, made of rough thick wood with an iron ring attached. Like my cat, I succumbed to my curiosity and pulled the ring. A creak and a thwap later, a small door opened and dust flew everywhere. After it cleared, it revealed a small underground pantry with one, perfect, plump sweet potato. The last tuber in Germantown.

I pulled out this ancient root, slathered it in oil in a bowl, wrapped in foil, and roasted it up! I dressed this lady up for a night on the town with me, with only beautiful accessories from the earth—caramelized onions, roasted yellow pepper, and a beautifully nourishing tahini sauce with black beans. An Umami of elements. Fire in the pepper, water from the beans. Air moving through the microwave as I finished up the cook, and of course, my potato from the earth. My worries melted away like the buttery sauce. I, Sarah, poured a glass of red wine just for myself, and got to be me, eating this delicious, abundant magical potato.

WHAT YOU'LL NEED:

1 sweet potato
1 yellow pepper
1 yellow onion
1 can of black beans
olive oil
salt and pepper

FOR THE SAUCE

1 tbsp of tahini
1 tbsp of soy sauce
4 tbsp of softened butter
2 cloves of garlic, minced
½ tbsp of maple syrup
salt and pepper
juice of a lemon

WHAT YOU'LL NEED TO DO:

1. Preheat the oven to 400°. Pierce the sweet potato and slather in olive oil, salt and pepper. Roast for about 20 - 30 minutes, or until the inside is cooked.
2. Over a gas burner, place yellow bell pepper and roast until it's black all over. Place in a paper bag and let it sit while you make the caramelized onions.
3. Meanwhile, slice the onion into ¼ inch pieces. Add to a preheated pan and saute with olive oil on medium heat for 4 - 6 minutes. Reduce heat. Add salt. As onions begin to soften and release their juices, stir occasionally to ensure nothing is burning. Saute until onions have reached a dark brown hue (15-20 minutes).
4. Wash any black off of the yellow bell pepper. Remove the seeds and the cap, and slice into ¼ inch strips.
5. Rinse the canned black beans and let drain.

MAKE THE TAHINI SAUCE:

6. In a bowl, mash together the tahini, soy sauce, butter, garlic and syrup until it's all incorporated. Add salt, pepper and lemon juice to taste. Put it on literally anything.

ASSEMBLE THE POTATO:

7. Cut open the sweet potato, layer in the black beans, then the caramelized onions and last the roasted yellow bell pepper. Finally, drizzle with tahini sauce. Enjoy with fresh herbs such as parsley or cilantro.

NOTES

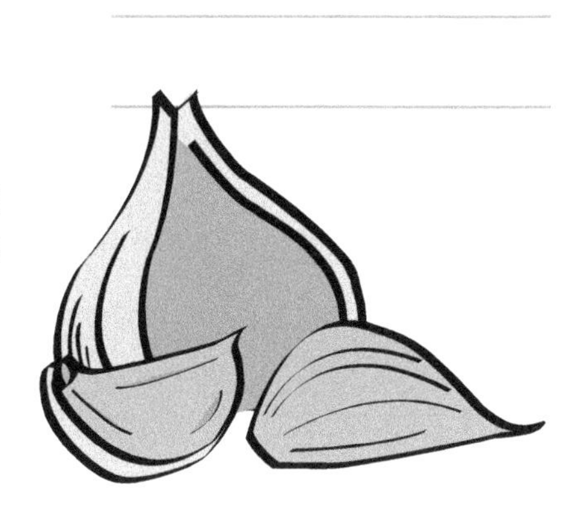

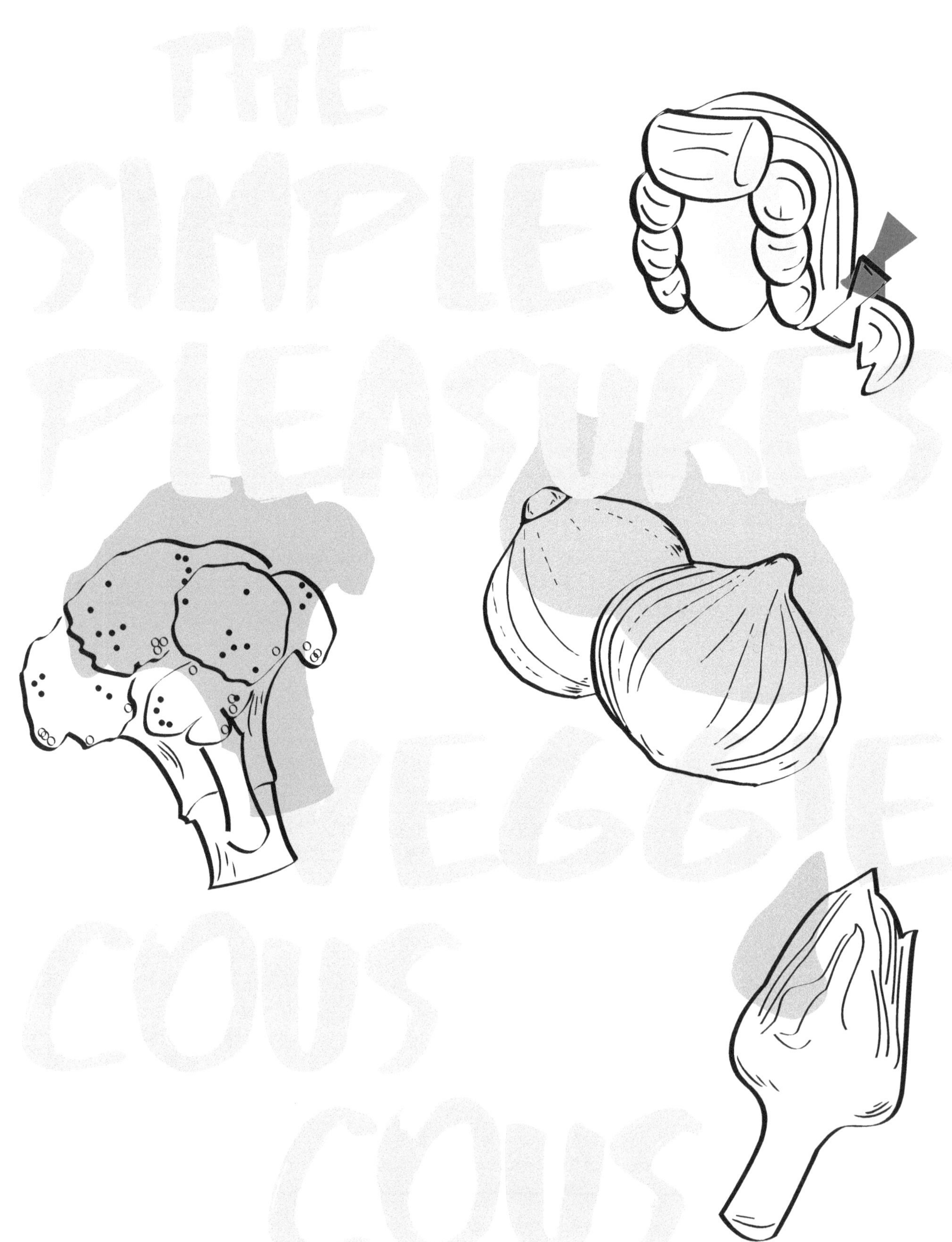
THE
SIMPLE
PLEASURES
VEGGIE
COUS
COUS

BY FRANNY & CONNOR & VANESSA

As a kid, pasta sprinkle was magic. In just a few shakes of this seasoning on your freshly cooked noodles, you had delicious pasta that would make Chef Boyardee sing. But I didn't want to eat pasta! I wanted to eat real American food: like bagel bites and mac and cheese. When I learned how I could use beautiful spices like parsley, oregano and basil, I was shocked to taste my old friend—pasta sprinkle—once again.

That's what inspired me to make this herby veggie dish that tastes like an afternoon on a Mediterranean riviera. Share this veggie-packed couscous with a friend—the Snoop Dogg to your Martha Stewart, perhaps? Improvising in the kitchen means getting silly sometimes, so don't be afraid to throw some parkour in while the couscous is boiling. And cleanup couldn't be easier: one bowl,
one pot, one pan. And that means more time for fun later. After your light dish, finish off the night with a punch made from an epic poem. Powdered wigs required

WHAT YOU'LL NEED:

FOR THE COUSCOUS:

1 ½ cup of couscous
2 tbs of olive oil
1 ¾ cup of veggie stock

FOR THE ROASTED VEGETABLES:

2 tbs olive oil
4 garlic cloves, diced
1 onion, diced
1 carrot, chopped
1 head of broccoli, (or 1 bag of frozen broccoli florets)
1-2 marinated artichoke hearts
1 15 oz can of chickpeas, drained and rinsed
juice of 1 lemon
1 tsp Italian seasoning
salt
black pepper, freshly ground

WHAT YOU'LL NEED TO DO:

1. Preheat the oven to 375°.
2. Chop up garlic and hearty vegetables—onion, carrots, and broccoli—to desired chunkiness. Then mix them up in big bowl with salt, pepper, olive oil, and plenty of pasta sprinkle—or Italian seasoning.
3. Toss mixture out onto a baking sheet and roast up until nice and caramelized.
4. Set salted water to boil and cook couscous to directions on your box. Swap in water for veggie stock if you'd like and add olive oil for extra richness.
5. Mix your cooked vegetables with the cooked couscous. Add chopped artichokes, chickpeas, and lemon juice.

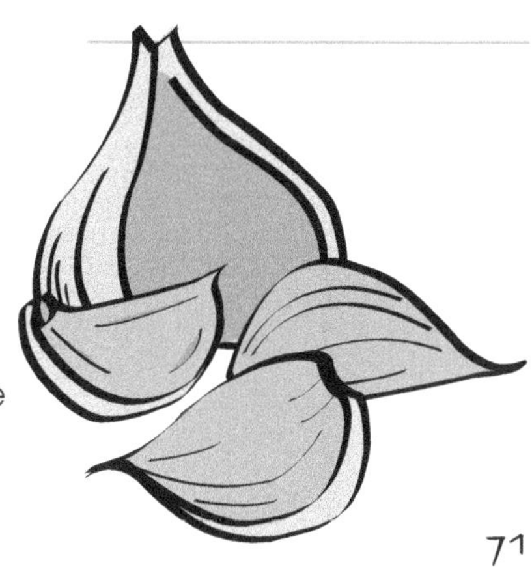

FOOL
PROOF
FANCY

Look, let's be honest: fancy home cooking can be tough. While we know that we first eat with our eyes, we've all had a very messy stew or chili that on first glance might look like horse meat but, with the first bite, a symphony of flavors and textures runs trills across our taste buds. A bowl of Cincinnati Chili Five Ways, for example, might look like a dog food slopped on top of soggy spaghetti with three more layers consisting of raw white onions, tepid pinto beans and fluffy mild cheese because... well that's what it is. But when you feel the side of your fork cut through the five layers (yes even the spaghetti, this isn't a twirling game) and you bring a tiny bite of each element to your lips, you realize: it just works. Looking down at your tower of carbs and meat and cheese, you appreciate the look because it just tastes so damn good. The taste of a dish can inform how you dress the dish up but never forget what truly makes a meal—the people you share it with.

Everyday home cooking is a gift but what about those special occasions when you want to go the extra mile? In this section, you'll find recipes for those little moments you choose to celebrate. Sometimes you just want to make something big and complicated to show someone you care. And sometimes that person is you learning how you can celebrate and love yourself through food. These moments could be the birthday fajitas that we made with our dear friend Greg or some self-love scallops for one with Megan, a new mom who we've known since she was our college classmate. Both of these dishes couldn't have looked more different, and yet both of the cooks were taking the time to give themselves a home cooked meal.

Food can be a celebration and how you choose to present it should be what looks good to you. If you've read the previous recipes, you'll have read about Colin and the barbecue sauce on his quesadillas. When Colin was plating his dish, he gave a generous drizzle of this delectable sauce all over his quesadilla. With a smile, he brought the plate up to the camera and said "It's just like a Dunkin Latte." We all love taking that extra step for ourselves. So next time you're plating that same old stir fry or pasta dish for a weeknight dinner, think about what you want to present and how you could make that night special.

RECIPES!

RIP BO SHRIMP KEBOBS WITH CAULIFLOWER RICE

BY FRANNY & CONNOR & SARAH & PETE

Like Salt and Pepper—the spices, not the band—Pete and Sarah have been inseparable since they first met. They're vast and numerous adventures have taken them across the globe. Whether it be London to Barcelona or Washington, DC to Martha's Vineyard, the destinations these jet setters landed on meant they were hardly ever sitting still. The only constant in their travels was their companionship. They knew that they always had a traveling buddy in the other.

On their latest adventure to Martha's Vineyard, they were strolling down the beaches when a Portuguese water dog bounded out of the dunes and into the water.

Sara turned to Pete and shouted, "I think that was Bo!"

"Bo who?" Pete said

"Bo Obama? The Obama dog?"

Without exchanging a word, they shot into the shallow waves and began to corral the obviously lost (and very expensive) dog. After many kissing noises and knee pats, they finally coaxed the ex-first pet out of the ocean. It was only then that a statuesque woman emerged on the scene with a broken collar in her hand.

Michelle Obama stood in the ocean breeze, nervously scanning the horizon for any sight of her beloved fluffy friend. Sara sent Pete to get her attention and then turned back to Bo with whom she was playing tug of war. In his furry jaws, Sara saw a shrimp net he had caught from an unsuspecting fisherman that was full of wriggly sea bugs.

"Thank you so much for saving Bo!" Michelle said. "To repay you, why don't you come over for dinner with Barack and me?

"But what could we cook?" Pete said

"I think I know," Sara said as she yanked the shrimp net out of Bo's mouth.

That night, they dined on this cauliflower rice bowl with za'atar shrimp. Made by the hand of the South Lawn Vegetable Garden Queen herself, this bowl satisfied Sara and Pete with veggies and crustaceans. As the two power couples said their goodbyes, Michelle squeezed Sara close and slipped a piece of paper into Sara's parka pocket. As soon as the front door shut behind them, Sara took the paper out, carefully unfolded it and found the recipe for this dish for her to cherish always.

WHAT YOU'LL NEED:

- 1 lb shrimp (19-20 count)
- 1 red bell pepper
- 2 tbsp olive oil
- leafy greens or lettuce
- ¼ cup fresh parsley, chopped
- salt and pepper
- 1 cauliflower head
- 2-3 garlic cloves
- red pepper flakes
- 1 carrot
- ½ tsp za'atar
- 1 lemon

WHAT YOU'LL NEED TO DO:

1. Wash off your cauliflower and cube up into 1 inch chunks, blitz it up to the texture of rice in your food processor.
2. Set a large pan on medium-low heat. Once at temperature, add about 2 tablespoons of olive oil and add your garlic and a pinch of red pepper flakes.
3. Dice some carrots and toss in the pan. Season with salt and pepper. Once soft, add the cauliflower, with about ½ cup of water to steam up the cauliflower. Cook off the water, adding more water if necessary, until the cauliflower rice is cooked to taste.
4. Roast your red pepper. You can do this with tongs over your gas flame, or broiled on high in an oven. Once charred up, put it in a paper bag to steam. Then, once cooled, peel the skin off the pepper. Chop up and set aside, add them to the cooked cauliflower dish. Squeeze lemon and add salt and pepper to taste.
5. Pat your shrimp dry with a paper towel. In a bowl, add the shrimp with a the 1/2 tsp of za'atar, salt, and pepper and toss until evenly coated. Skewer the shrimp and then set aside. Heat up your grill or grill pan, oiling if necessary.
6. Grill the shrimp until it turns translucent. Pull off heat and squeeze some lemon on top. Serve the skewers with the cauliflower rice, cover with your greens, fresh parsley, and more sliced lemon.

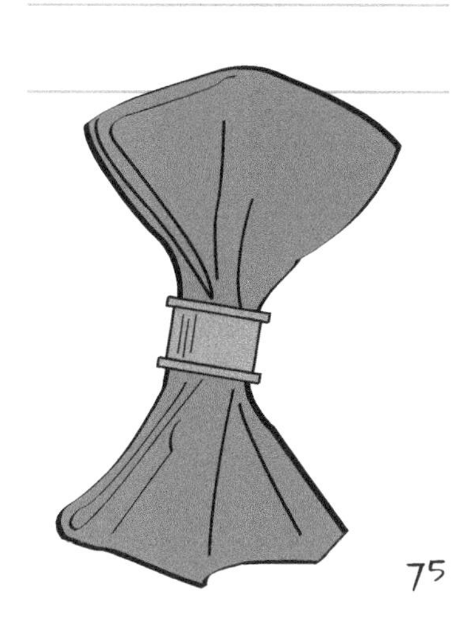

MY BIG FAT GREEK EX-BOYFRIEND'S MEZZE PLATE

BY FRANNY & CONNOR & DAVEN & MYRIAM

I woke up in Santorini, heartbroken. My veil was torn to shreds and my left heel split in two. I was a sorry sight to look at as I cried my salty tears into the Mediterranean. Dimitrios, my hunky Greek boyfriend, had told me to meet him in the cradle of civilization to cement our nuptials. But when I arrived in the Greek Isles dressed like Fran Drescher in the wedding episode of *The Nanny,* Dimitrios was nowhere to be found.

Then, there was hope. Through my tears, I saw her emerging from the hills of Mt Olympus: my friend Daven who was nude from the waist up and munching on a tasty salad with ground beef, olives and pita bread.

"Daven, what are you doing here?

"Whaaaaaaaat?" Daven said "I've always been here. C'mon Myriam! Let's get out of here."

I dried my eyes, and took her hand as she offered me a bite of meat with her other. We flew back to Baltimore together. It was there that, just as Daven had opened her arms to me, I was welcomed by the embrace of her family.

Now, I've found the love of my life in her brother, John. Our lives are much different now: Daven usually wears a shirt. We cook together. pizzas and salads and brinner—which is breakfast for dinner for those who don't know. And we still make this mezze plate even though Daven can't remember where she first found it.

The taste of the well spiced beef with the fresh spinach and orchestra of veggies reminds us that we all found each other. It also shows us how we can always come home when things look their darkest.

WHAT YOU'LL NEED:

- 1 lb ground beef, room temp
- 1 red onion, minced
- 1 tsp chopped flat leaf parsley
- ½ tsp cayenne pepper
- ½ tsp ground cinnamon
- ½ tsp ground coriander
- ⅛ tsp ground nutmeg
- 1 bag of spinach
- Iceberg or butter lettuce (for lettuce wraps)
- salt and pepper to taste
- 1 cucumber
- 1 tomato
- 2 carrots
- 1 red pepper
- 1 cup Greek yogurt
- ¼ cup fresh dill, chopped

WHAT YOU'LL NEED TO DO:

1. Mince up the red onion. Half of this you'll cook up with the beef and the other half you'll add raw to your platter.
2. Put a large pan on medium high heat. Once up to temperature, add a 1 tablespoon olive oil and add the red onion for the beef. Once soft, add the meat. As it cooks, break up the meat in the pan, getting a nice brown on it.
3. Once most of the liquid has cooked off, add your dried spices (cayenne pepper, cinnamon, ground coriander, nutmeg, salt, and pepper). Add to the platter in a bowl.
4. Assemble your platter: Cut up the peppers and carrots into matchsticks, slice up your tomatoes, and add them, along with the spinach, to your mezze platter.
5. Chop up a handful of dill and cube up your cucumbers. Pat them dry with a towel. In a medium bowl, mix Greek yogurt, the dill, the cucumbers, and a few glugs of olive oil to make a nice tzatziki to add to your platter.
6. Serve the whole thing together, with hummus, lettuce wraps, pita or pita chips. If you have it, add olives or pickles. Use your fingers to make delicious bites in whatever combination you like!

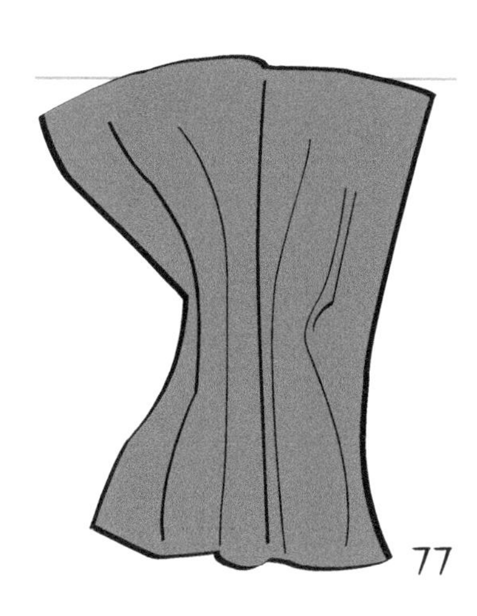

BY FRANNY & CONNOR & GREG

Greg's birthday is always a special day. Not only is it a day when we celebrate the birth of an extraordinary man, writer, and friend. It is also Cinco de Mayo. This ultimate day of celebration is always full of love, joy, and booze! Now that we are in our very very very very early 30's, it's important to deny the aging process by continuing to drink at the same pace as we always have. But, because we are wiser, we also make sure that we are heading off that hangover with a very filling spicy meal.

Greg, the Birthday Man, and Mandy, the Birthday Mandy, knew they wanted to celebrate Greg's second quarantine birthday with a fun and easy Mexican-inspired dish. Unfortunately, they had pre-gamed this cook hard! While Mandy was searching through the mystery Tupperware leftovers, Greg paraded by with two perfectly marbled steaks on his belly, shouting "Meat Man!"

"Hey babe," Mandy said, "why don't you give me those steaks and we can make some delicious fajitas.

"Are you sure?" Greg said, "These steaks have been on my belly for several days."

"Several days?" Mandy asked, peeling them off his belly. "You've only been dancing around like this for 20 minutes. And where did you even get these steaks?"

"Don't worry babe, it's birthday steaks!" Greg said with a drunken grin.

"OK, it's your day," Mandy said with a sigh, "Plus these steaks are the perfect temperature for cooking!"

So, she and Greg whipped up steak fajitas with cilantro cream and refried beans. Serve on chairs with pitcher after pitcher of margaritas. Lean back on your couch and eat with your plate on your belly. Enjoy this recipe, infused with all the glorious bits of Greg, the Birthday Man. These fajitas are passionate, joyful, fiercely loyal and empathetic. They have a lust for life, and all things delicious just like Greg. And they also tell a great fucking story.

WHAT YOU'LL NEED:

- 1 yellow onion, sliced
- 1 green bell pepper
- 1 lb, hanger steak
- 3 cloves, garlic
- ½ tsp cumin
- ¼ tsp chili powder
- salt and pepper
- tortillas

FOR THE CILANTRO YOGURT 'CREMA':

- 2 tbsp fresh cilantro, roughly chopped
- 1 jalapeno, seeded and diced
- ¼ cup yogurt

NOTES

WHAT YOU'LL NEED TO DO:

1. Warm up the cold steak by placing it on your belly until it comes to room temperature. Add salt, pepper and chili powder until well seasoned. Cut the steak into one inch strips.
2. Slice the onion and green bell pepper. Dice the garlic. Add oil to a heated cast iron skillet over medium high heat. When oil begins to shimmer, add in onion, green bell pepper, garlic, salt, pepper and cumin. Cook til vegetables begin to loosen.
3. Add the steak to the hot pan and cook until steak is cooked medium rare—130° to 140° as registered on a meat thermometer. Remove skillet from heat.
4. While the steak rests, prepare the cilantro yogurt 'crema.' Dice jalapenos fine, making sure to remove the seeds and any excess pith. Add ¼ of yogurt to the bowl with the jalapenos. Rip up cilantro leaves and add to the bowl along with the juice of half a lime. Stir and add salt to taste.
5. Warm up your tortillas in the oven or on the stove if you have gas burners. Serve with refried black beans if you wish and as tacos with the crema slathered on top.

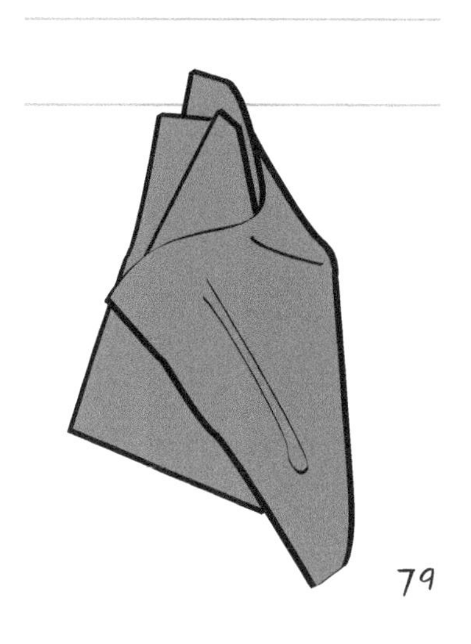

HOW TOM AND ASHLEY GOT THEIR GROOVE BACK UNDER THE TUSCAN STYLE STEAK SALAD

BY FRANNY & CONNOR & TOM & ASHLEY

Let's face it, 2020 was a wash. So many canceled celebrations, graduations, and weddings! But Tom and Ashley didn't let the memory of a terrible year stand in the way of their beautiful Tuscan Honeymoon—which they pounced upon at the first chance that it was safe to travel.

On their first morning in Tuscany, they awoke at four in the morning to take their baskets to the fresh olive groves. There, they set to work, grabbing up as many briny berries as they could. As they were walking back to their villa, arms full of delicious olives, they happened upon an old man named Alfredo who sold produce on the side of the road. Ashley and Tom grabbed some herbs, onions and fresh greens from Alfredo whose farm lay just behind a copse of cyprus trees. He welcomed them back to his farm where they met his prized cow, Bertita. Unfortunately for their new friend, however, it was time for her to go to the butcher's block and the happy couple took a piece of her with them home to their rented villa.

After a delicious wine tasting, they made this Tuscan herbed steak with a fresh Mediterranean salad. Bertita's beautiful meat released its juices into the pan and made for a perfect sauce for the dish. They served it over Alfredo's fresh produce—a beautiful salad crisp as the twilighting Mediterranean air. As the sun set, they took a bite of steak, a sip of wine (or was it a sip of wine and a bite of steak) and looked out into the beautiful Italian countryside. They looked at each other and clinked their glasses together. Here's for their new happy life together.

WHAT YOU'LL NEED:

salt and pepper
cuts of steak
(skirt or flank steak is fine here. whatever is in your budget!)
2 tbsp olive oil
1/4 cup red wine
sprig of rosemary
clove of garlic
2 tbsp butter
lemon juice

SALAD

salad
greens (arugula, spinach, whatever you've got)
lemon
shallots
shaved Pecorino Romano or Parmesan

NOTES

WHAT YOU'LL NEED TO DO:

1. One day ahead, pat down the meat with paper towels, and salt and pepper generously, and return to the fridge. An hour before you cook your steak, pull the meat out to come to room temperature. Pat down one more time with a paper towel.
2. Heat a medium sized, thick pan on medium high. Once at temperature, add 2 tablespoons of olive oil.
3. Add the steak and sear, cooking for 3 minutes, flip and cook for another 3 minutes. Throw some rosemary in the pan. Then, flip every 1 minute, then 30 seconds until cooked to desired doneness. (I recommend Medium Rare (130°-140°F). In between each flip, rub the side-up-side with butter, garlic, and rosemary.
4. Pull the steak off the heat and let sit for a least 10 minutes. Set pan aside.
5. Throw together a quick salad of greens, shallots, lemon juice and olive oil. Shave cheese on top. Slice steaks thinly, across the grain.
6. Mix the juice released from the steak into the pan with a squeeze of lemon and some butter, to taste. Top the steak with your delicious juice, more lemon and rosemary, and serve with salad.

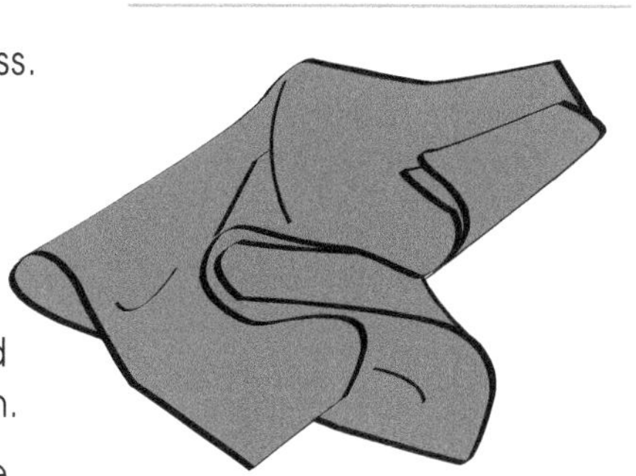

SLAM
MING
MOON
YAY OR
SALMON
MEUNIERE

BY FRANNY & CONNOR & KARI

When I was a young girl, I did not cook. It always scared me to step into the kitchen and look into my small sink with my inadequate faucet.

That all changed when I studied in Paris. It was Spring Break and I thought "Wouldn't it be fun to go into the country?" And so I took the bus to the countryside of southern France. As I traveled, the soothing movement of the bus and the warmth of the French sun lulled me to sleep as my compatriots and I lurched over the rolling hills. When I woke up, I was past my stop! And all my stuff was gone!

I stepped off the bus in unfamiliar territory, and found myself in a quaint one stoplight French town that was out in the middle of nowhere. Unfortunately, I did not speak the local dialect but an adorable old couple found me sitting on the side of the road, lost and overwhelmed. They brought me to their home which was a short walk from where they came upon me. They sat me down in their kitchen, and made me coffee. I'll never forget watching the bus dust off my face and hands in their big beautiful kitchen sink. Once, I was all washed up, they could innately sense my hunger—most French folks have this hidden talent. Immediately, they set to teaching me how to make this Slamming Moon Yay. (Like I said, I didn't speak the dialect, so I didn't know how to spell the name of the dish.)

Now, I am a grown ass woman who is a boss in the kitchen. I wash my hands in my big beautiful sink in my big beautiful kitchen. To this day, I still think of Pierre and Dominique and remember the smell of thyme and garlic in brown butter.

And THIS is that recipe.

NOTES

WHAT YOU'LL NEED:

- 1 lb salmon, cut into two fillets
- 2 tbsp butter
- ¼ cup all purpose flour
- 1 tsp capers, roughly chopped
- zest and juice of 1 lemon
- thyme
- salt and pepper
- ¼ tsp garlic powder (optional)

WHAT YOU'LL NEED TO DO:

1. Preheat oven to 425°.
2. In a shallow dish, whisk together salt, pepper and garlic powder if using.
3. If your salmon has skin, remove skin. Pat salmon fillet dry and dredge through the flour mixture. Dust off any excess flour.
4. Melt the butter in a pan that can go into the oven. A cast iron skillet works but a lighter pan such as a stainless steel would work better.
5. Once butter is foaming, add salmon face down into the pan. Do not disturb for three minutes or until sides and top are opaque.
6. Flip salmon. Add zest of lemon, lemon juice, capers and thyme to the pan. Mix slightly.
7. Place the pan in the oven and bake for six minutes.
8. Garnish with an egg cooked to your liking and serve with a side salad.

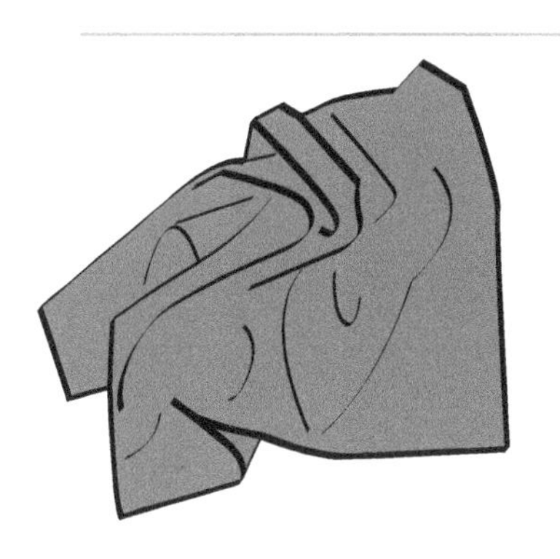

SOLO SCALLOP SELF-ACTUALIZATION- A JOURNEY IN SELF LOVE

BY FRANNY & CONNOR & MEGAN

Megan loves the sea. Throughout her childhood, her family was always at the shore—staying in converted barns right off the beaches of the Atlantic Ocean. Her time there was always full of fishing, soaking up the sun and cooking delicious meals from their catch of the day. As a young girl, the first thing she ever cooked was a pan fried trout—flipping it with ease like a pancake.

As she grew into a young adult, the Atlantic was swapped for the Mediterranean as she frequently visited the Italian countryside on holiday with her mother, Laura. The two of them were always off on an adventure through the various Italian provinces, sampling the local cuisine. It was during their time in the city of Pescara when a dubious waiter brought Laura and her a five course meal pulled directly from the sea. They gobbled up the feast with gusto. Except for the scallops which Megan took the
time to savor as their inimitable texture melted through her mouth.

Now, as she grows into a mother herself, fresh fish has often been substituted for potato dinners, and the sea, which had inspired adventure, replaced by a home full to the brim with love. Yet there are still times where she yearns for the flavor and the fervor of the sea. So, when she's home alone, and tending to herself, she pulls out this recipe that reminds her how far she's come and to where her ship is still sailing.

WHAT YOU'LL NEED:

½ lb pasta (recommended spaghetti or angel hair)
¼ lb fresh scallops*, (or thawed frozen)
2 to 3 tbsp olive oil
½ cup white wine
2 tbsp butter
salt and pepper
¼ cup fresh parsley, chopped
juice of 1 lemon

*This is typically four to five scallops

NOTES

WHAT YOU'LL NEED TO DO:

1. Take your scallops out of the fridge about 15 to 20 minutes before cooking so that they come to room temperature. Dry off your scallops with a paper towel, then salt and pepper them.
2. Start your pasta pot: fill a pot with 2 to 3 quarts of water salted like the sea. Bring it to a boil and cook the pasta as directed by the box. After you dump in your pasta, set a pan on a separate burner to medium low.
3. Once the pan is warm, add 2 to 3 tablespoons of olive oil and lightly pan fry the scallops. These should cook up very quickly and turn white/opaque—30 seconds per side. As they cook, pour in about ½ cup of wine, squeeze half of lemon in, and a few pads of butter to create a pan sauce.
4. When there are about 2 to 3 minutes left on the pasta, remove the scallops from the pan and transfer to a dish. Drain the pasta, and finish cooking in the scallop pan, adding some pasta water to keep the dish from drying out.
5. Once the pasta has soaked up all the beautiful flavors, and is cooked to your taste, pull off heat and top with scallops, chopped parsley, and/or more lemon or oil. Serve immediately.

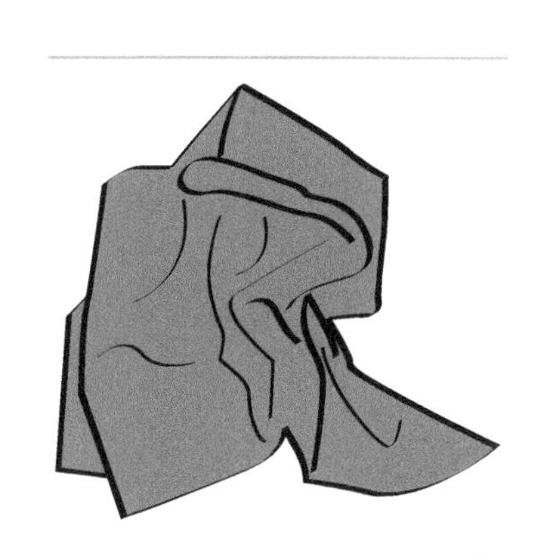

Francesca Chilcote is a freelance teaching artist, actor, and theatre-maker based in Washington, DC. She holds a BA in Theatre from the The College of William and Mary (Williamsburg, VA) and an MFA in Physical Theatre from the Accademia dell'Arte (Arezzo, IT), where she studied commedia dell'arte under Maestro Marcello Bartoli. She, along with Kathryn Zoerb, serves as a Co-Artistic Director for Faction of Fools Theatre Company (www.factionoffools.org), a commedia company in DC. She also regularly performs in Faction's shows as a company member. She teaches clown, commedia, and devising at the Performing and Visual Arts magnet program at Annapolis High School in Anne Arundel County, MD.

She is also a certified teacher of the Elemental Body Alignment System (EBAS). Her work as a translator is featured in The Routledge Companion to Commedia dell'arte.

More info at
www.francescamariechilcote.com

Connor Hogan is a performer, creator and educator with over a decade of experience in theater. As an actor and director, he has worked at theaters across the country to include the Folger Theater, Constellation Theater Company, WSC Avant Bard, and Theater Unspeakable. As a deviser, he explores theatrical questions with a wild physicality in order to excavate a truth. His most recent works include Gilligan Gigs Again and The Usual, which was a part of his thesis performance in 2019. He is a graduate of the Pig Iron Theatre School as well as the Moscow Art Theatre American School. Through collaboration and play, he seeks to bring together folks of all backgrounds and uplift voices of the marginalized.

More info at
www.connordinary.com

THANK YOU! THANK YOU! THANK YOU!

We are eternally grateful to everyone who made this crazy cookbook possible. This was a true labor of love. The whole idea for the show, and eventually this cookbook, began as a joke we would tell each other. So we are ecstatic to see this joke not only turn into a show but lead to our first published cookbook. First off, thank you to every single audience member who let us into their kitchens and digitally raid their pantries. This cookbook would have been a failure if it wasn't for each of you, your stories, your hunger and your head-scratching ingredients.

Thank you to our play testers–Christy Sexton, Liz Larson, Sarah Gardner, John Hawthorne, Chris Stinson, Katelin Lee, and Mary Myers. You all helped us shape the performance, and prepared us to take on this wild idea. And to offer this generosity up while everyone else was just trying to survive was a gift that we are still grateful for to this day.

We'd also like to thank Debi Belt, her Graphic Design class at the Cleveland Institute of Art, and our lead concept designer, Hannah Cabbell. If Debi had not approached us to use our performance as an assignment for her class, we wouldn't have even known where to start. Debi's class gave us a plethora of inspiration and we're so happy to have gotten the chance to work with Hannah on her design. Thank you to Michael Manfroni for his editing and incredible eye for detail. If he had not caught it, there may be no shrimp in the shrimp kebobs and the shakshuka might leave dents in your pan. Thank you, and we love you.

Finally, thank you for reading this! We hope that you've learned something about your cooking style, and how you use the ingredients laying around your kitchen. If you want to stay in touch, or you have any questions, feel free to reach out to us through our websites.

In Food and Friendship,

FRANCESCA CHILCOTE & CONNOR HOGAN

Milton Keynes UK
Ingram Content Group UK Ltd.
UKHW051846040823
426284UK00004B/132